FAITH OR FATHERHOOD?
BISHOP DUNBOYNE'S DILEMMA

The Story of John Butler, Catholic Bishop of Cork 1763-1787

By the Same Author

Ireland and the Holy Land: Irish Links with the Levant from the Earliest Times (C.
   Goodliffe Neale, Alcester & Dublin, 1974)
In Quest of an Heir (Tower Books, Cork, 1978)
The O'Connell Memorial Church, Cahirciveen (Cahirciveen Parish, 1984)
Botany Bay: The Story of the convicts Transported from Ireland to Australia 1791-1853
   (Mercier Press, Cork, 1987)
Looking Back: Aspects of History County Kildare (Leinster Leader, Naas, 1988)
Guide to Kildare and West Wicklow (Leinster Leader, Naas, 1991)
Kildare: Saints, Soldiers & Horses (Leinster Leader, Naas, 1991)
*A Most Delightful Station: The British Army on the Curragh of Kildare, Ireland, 1855-
   1922* (Collins Press, Cork, 1996)
Peerless Punchestown: 150 Years of Glorious tradition (with Raymond Smith) (Sport-
   ing Books, Publishers, Dublin, 2000)

Faith or Fatherhood?

Bishop Dunboyne's Dilemma

The Story of John Butler, Catholic Bishop of Cork 1763-1787

CON COSTELLO

The Woodfield Press

This book was typeset in Ireland by
Gough Typesetting Services for
THE WOODFIELD PRESS
17 Jamestown Square, Inchicore, Dublin 8, Ireland.
Web: http://myhome.iolfree.ie/~woodfield
E-mail: terri.mcdonnell@ireland.com

House editor
Paul Candon

Index
Thérèse Carrick

The catalogue record for this title
is available from the British Library.

ISBN 0-9528453-9-3

Printed in Ireland
by Genprint Limited

Dedication

To the memory of the many members of my family who faithfully served the Church over the last two centuries

John 22nd Lord Dunboyne's Paternal Family

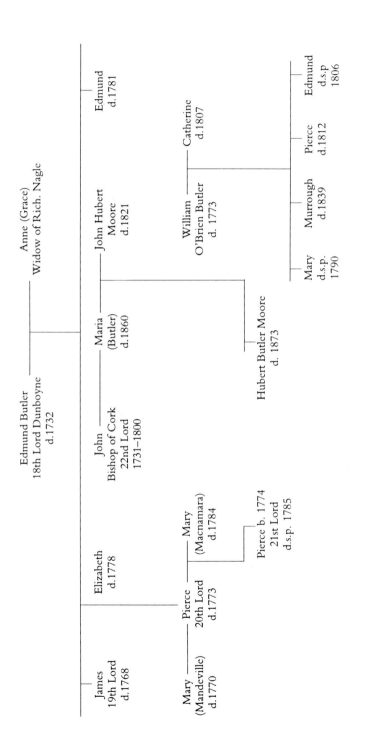

Contents

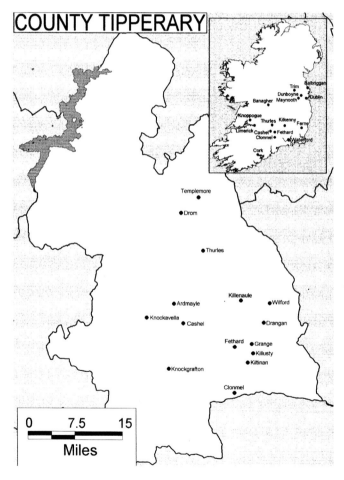

Map of Ireland and of County Tipperary showing places associated with the Butler family

List of Illustrations

Foreword

Peter de Rosa

I first heard the story forty years ago. In the late 18th century, John Butler, the elderly, bewigged and one-eyed Bishop of Cork renounced his See to marry his young cousin, Maria. In so doing, he broke his vows and professed his unbelief in, among other things, the Real Presence. It was, as a Dublin newspaper of the time put it, "one of the most singular events which has happened for many centuries".

I had to wait much longer for the full story as told by Con Costello in his fascinating book, *In Quest of an Heir*. I happened to be writing my own *Vicars of Christ: the Dark Side of the Papacy*. Con Costello's researches provided me with a glittering tale made up in equal measure of scandal, fun and profound poignancy.

Two centuries after Bishop Butler made his proposal to Maria, Ireland was shaken by another revelation in what became known as the Bishop Casey affair.

Both Butler and Casey had a touching affection for the Church of their childhood, both achieved much in their ministry, both finally repented of what they had done. But the differences between them are equally significant.

Butler seems to have been touchingly naïve. Having inherited the title Lord Dunboyne, he was keen to perpetuate his line by having an heir, even if it meant marrying a Protestant lady to acquire one. Trusting to his famous name and lineage, he expected the Pope of the day, Pius VI, to dispense him from his vow of celibacy and validate his marriage. His petition was, naturally, turned down. He was accused of treachery, of being a modern Pharaoh whose heart had been hardened, a latter-day Henry VIII destined surely for the hot place. And, sadly, an heir eluded him.

In time to come, Butler and Casey will doubtless be bracketed together as the two men who did most harm to the institutional side of the Catholic Church in Ireland. I suspect, however, that further generations will look benignly on them. If, as is said, tragedy is only undeveloped comedy, the time is not far off when most people will simply laugh at the pleasure their unusual stories afford.

I recommend Con Costello's book. It is very well researched and written; its theme is increasingly relevant to Ireland's present situation. And, dare I say it, it not only has many lessons to teach, it reads like a charming novel.

Preface

by the 28th Lord Dunboyne

The predecessor of mine who is the subject of this book excited strong feelings in his day. Some believe his soul is still frizzling in hell, and long has he stood in need of an objective appraisal. But where are particulars of him to be found? As long ago as 1879 that question was published in *Notes and Queries* and it went unanswered. Now, however, Col. Con Costello provides this cornucopia of the fruits of his research on the subject and, with chapter and verse, supplies the answer to a century-old question.

To have gathered the material facts and presented them dispassionately can have been no easy task. In the beginning, next to nothing is known of John's early childhood which must have been in Ireland, or of his education, which was almost certainly on the European continent.

In order to come to terms with the ensuing drama, it is essential to have some idea of the year of his birth in particular. Yet there is no direct evidence on the point. It is purely a matter of inference. No less an authority than *The Complete Peerage* placed his birth-year "about 1720". But that is inaccurate and misleading. He cannot have been born before 1730. For Monsieur L.V. Pauchet has recently uncovered in the *Archives de la Guerre* a dossier, labelled "Pierre Butler", which gives the precise date of birth of John's elder brother, Pierce, as 16 April 1729. At the other end of the time-bracket, John is unlikely to have been born after 1731, because his father died in November 1732 and had after John, at least one younger child, Edmund. Furthermore, as Col. Costello, reminds us, John himself swore in 1758 that he was 27. So there is every indication that Canon Burke was correct to state in *Irish Priests in Penal Times* that John was born in 1731.

His career was unusual at every turn. At an early age he somehow lost an eye. When Pope Clement XIII nominated him bishop at the age of 32, it was the result of almost the last interference by the Stuarts in Episcopal appointments. Then again, a one-eyed bishop was something of an oddity. So even his appearance was out of the ordinary.

No portrait of him seems to have survived. The only one known to have existed used to hang in Knoppogue Castle, Co. Clare, when I was an infant, and such information as I have of its fate is perhaps worth publishing, especially as strenuous efforts have been made to trace the picture for a national collection in Dublin. In 1927, an error led to its inclusion in an auction at which it was bought by a couple of family-conscious sisters, Miss Anna, and Miss Henrietta Butler of nearby Castle Crine. In her generosity, Anna, the survivor of the two, resolved to return the unique portrait to my father, then living in England; and shortly before her death in 1939 she arranged with him for her gift to be sent to him. It was packed up for the purpose and put in an outhouse at Castle Crine, to await despatch. But a lad, unaware that the case contained anything of value, used it "to deposit a load of chicken-feed"! The picture was consequently a write-off. Ireland, alas, has suffered more than her share of such losses. As Goethe put it, "what Man destroys in a minute, Eternity cannot restore".

In 1785, the coronet and the mitre which John found so incompatible came to be conjoined in him. He was then 54 and had been Catholic Bishop of Cork for no less than 23 years. The coronet he was assuming, by inheritance from his eleven-year-old nephew, was one of the most ancient in the peerage of Ireland. There had been successive Lords of Dunboyne ever since the 12th century. Early in the 14th century, the barony had passed through an heiress, named Synolda, to the Butler family and it has remained in that family even longer than the historic earldom of Ormond. John was not at all sure who his heir-male was. As Lord Dunboyne, he not unnaturally wanted to beget an heir. But as priest, he was prohibited from committing matrimony. He was anxious to secure the survival of his temporal heritage, if possible without in any way impugning the spiritual authority to which he was subject. Wishful thinking seems to have led him to imagine that, once divested of his priesthood, he would be permitted to marry. But it was a grave miscalculation. Although he tendered his resignation both as parish priest of St. Mary's in the city of Cork and as bishop of the diocese, the expected dispensation did not arrive. Instead, Pope Pius VI warned him, in no uncertain terms, of the consequences of his "concubinage". Meanwhile, in the knowledge that he was not getting any younger, John had gone too far. He had already, probably irrevocably, bound himself to marry. He was in a tangle and, in his dilemma, he cut the Gordian Knot by becoming a Protestant, at any rate, ostensibly. At heart, he may have remained a Catholic, for he was never more than lukewarm to his adopted Church and not only was his posthumous contribution to the Catholics substantial but it is also on record that he was subscribing three guineas to the Society of Catholics in Ireland on 25 April 1793. Another consideration which may, or may not, have influenced him was that his self-imposed spiritual exile offered distinct material advantages to a man of property like himself, in much the same way as being a tax exile might benefit a modern Dives. Nonetheless, John's recantation, read at Clonmel on 17 August 1787, was, and remains, the sole authenticated instance of the apostasy of a member of the Irish hierarchy.

There has been in more recent times a trite quip that John was more heir-minded than heir-conditioned. Many a true word is spoken in jest. At all events, no son of his was to survive him. Yet one cannot but feel sorry for him in the evening of his life, without "that which should accompany old age, as honour, love, obedience, troops of friends". Even the companionship of his much younger wife cooled. She never deserted him; but day after day and night after night for over five years he met her only at meals until death came to him, as a merciful release for them both.

She survived him by sixty years. Through her second marriage, she became ancestress of Field-Marshal Sir Claude Auchinleck, Sir Patrick Skipwith and numerous others of such names as Aldridge, Beaver, Butson, Eyre, Hopkins, Kemp, Leighton, Miller, Moore, Negretti, Newton, Nicoll, Peshall, Webber and White. They stretch to the Antipodes.

Different readers of this book will form different impressions of John. After all, his title to lasting fame is not really to be found in the drama of his transient apostasy. It resides much more in the solid contribution he made to the promotion of Catholic education within Ireland. In serving posterity so well, he was acting in the best traditions of his family. All three Butler Archbishops of Cashel in the 18th century had been dedicated to the same cause; Christopher, Archbishop 1712-1757, had early in his episcopate in Penal Days, established a seminary in Cashel to train aspirants to the priesthood; James, Archbishop 1757-1774, issued, in the month of his consecration, a *Pastoral* in Latin to regulate the examination of candidates for order or jurisdiction, and continued Christopher's good work; and James, Archbishop 1774-1791, was similarly occupied, in addition to introducing the Ursuline nuns to Thurles and bequeathing £2000 for the foundation of the Presentation Convent there. In the same tradition did John munificently endow Maynooth. Not for nothing are certain members of that great college still called 'Dunboyners'. The good John did was not interred with his bones.

In the end was no cause for wailing or gnashing of teeth but an abiding hope - the hope enshrined in Proverbs, xiv, 27, whence came the treasured motto of the Dunboynes:

Timor Domini Fons Vitae

Chronology

1801 Courts hearing opens, *Catherine O'Brien v. Maynooth College.*
      Lady Dunboyne, aged 36, marries John Hubert Moore.
1802 Court case transferred to Trim Assizes. Fr. Gahan committed to Gaol.
      Parties agree to endeavour to reach an amicable settlement.
1805 Lady Dunboyne, wife of John Hubert Moore, gives birth to a son.
1808 An Act passed to enable the Trustees of Maynooth to compromise the
      suit.
1813 Dunboyne House, Maynooth, built.
1820 Constitution for Dunboyne House drawn up.
1822 Lady Dunboyne again widowed.
1823 Bishop Butler's nephew fails in attempt to claim title.
1827 Legal claimant to title established by James Butler.
1859 Mrs. O'Brien Butler dies.
1860 Lady Dunboyne dies.
1935 Duboyne vault opened. Coffins identified.
1964 Eoin O'Mahony recounts rumours from Rome.

Abbreviations

Healy, *Maynooth*   Most Rev. John Healy, *Maynooth College, its Centenary History,* 1895.
Renchan, *Collections*   L. F. Renehan, *Collections on Irish Church History* (ed. D. McCarthy), 2 vols. 1861, 1874.
Walsh, *Nagle*   T.J. Walsh, *Nano Nagle and the Presentation Sisters,* 1959.

PERIODICALS

Butler Jn.   *Journal of the Butler Society*
Coll. Hib.   *Collectanea Hibernica*
Cork Hist. Arch. Jn.   Cork Historical and Archaeological Society Journal
Galway Arch. Soc. Jn. Journal of the Galway Archaeological and Historical Society
Rep. Novum   Reportorium Novum

Acknowledgments

Grateful appreciation to the 28th Lord Dunboyne for his continuing interest in this material, for his suggestions and corrections, and for his valuable Preface. Sincere thanks to Peter de Rossa for his encouragement, and his apt Foreword. I remain indebted to the many other people who, over two decades ago, assisted me in my research, and who are mentioned in the acknowledgments to *In Quest of an Heir*. Thanks to Maeve for her drawing of the Dunboyne Shield, to Anne Fitzsimons and to Denis and Con William for their respective skills.

Con Costello

Tullig, Naas.
Holy Thursday, 2000.

CHAPTER ONE

Bishop of Cork 1763–1785

The advent of the Georgian era in Ireland saw many changes in the social and religious life of the nation; after the devastations of the 17th century the country now entered a period of comparative calm. While trade restrictions severely hampered commercial life, the bulk of the people, dependant on agriculture, survived in bucolic penury. Frequent famines failed to control an ever-increasing population, and the several foreign visitors who recorded their impressions of the Irish scene were unanimous in their observations of the degradation of the peasantry.

There was another side to the picture. The harsh application of some of the Penal Laws relating to the practice of Roman Catholic observance had fallen into disuse; Mass was said openly, though usually in a ruined church or secular building. In the second quarter of the 18th century the building of chapels commenced, and by the middle years the hierarchy, for the first time since the Reformation, was at full strength.

Instead of being absorbed in the suppression of the majority faith, many of the country's ruling class were preoccupied with the embellishment of their estates. Few buildings of architectural distinction had been erected in Ireland in the preceding century; now huge Italianate mansions erupted in the damp, green landscape. The building of Castletown, in Co. Kildare, was commenced in 1722, while one of the first of the great Dublin buildings, the new House of Parliament, was built seven years later.

Despite this apparent affluence and liberalism the country was still plagued with violent contrasts: a beggarly peasantry observed the creation of the vast country houses. Any Catholic family, which had succeeded by devious means in retaining some of its wealth, property and position, found it necessary to send its sons abroad to be educated. Young men wishing to become priests studied in one of the Irish colleges on the continent before returning home to embark on a vocation which was still a hazardous one. As late as 1766 Father Nicholas Sheehy, from Clogheen, Co. Tipperary was tried at Clonmel on a trumped-up agrarian murder charge. Found guilty under the martial laws then in vogue, he was executed.

What reaction Fr Sheehy's death caused on Rt Rev. Dr. John Butler, Bishop of Cork, we do not know. As a former parish priest of Ardmayle, in the same archdiocese as the executed priest, Butler must have known Fr Sheehy person-

Anne, née Grace, wife of Edmund, 18th Lord Dunboyne, and mother of Bishop John Butler of Cork

ally, though he may not have shared his views on the possible solutions to the land disturbances.

Butler, like many of the hierarchy of the period, came from a landed family. He was the third son of the 18th Lord Dunboyne, of Grange, near Fethard, Co. Tipperary. This branch of an ancient Norman family had remained Catholic, and during John Butler's student days a distant Ormonde relative occupied the See of Cashel.[1] At the age of nineteen Butler had decided on a career in the church, unlike his brothers Pierce and Edmund who were soldiering in France. John Butler travelled to the Irish College in Rome via Cadiz, Genoa and Leghorn;

---

[1] *Com. Peerage*, 1916, iv, 519. PRO MS 840, No. 94.

The Irish College in Rome which John Butler attended

following his arrival in the Via degli Ibernesi the student from Tipperary faded from the records until 1755. During those years he also attended lectures at Propaganda Fide, a fact which was to be among his recommendations for the bishopric in 1763.

Although an account of Butler's progress through the college is not now available it would seem that he did not live a completely sedentary student life. Due to an accident of some sort he had received an injury which resulted in the loss of his left eye, and in later years when his character was being subjected to scrutiny it was believed that he engaged in some disreputable escapade, likely a duel, in which he was injured. If his conduct had been disreputable it did not prevent his advancement in Holy Orders, though the absence of an eye could be an impediment to ordination. Two cardinals were appointed to examine the candidate and found him satisfactory, though dispensed *super defectu in oculo*.[2]

The Patriarch of Constantinople, Ferdinand Mary de Rubis, vicegerent of Rome, administered Tonsure to Butler and a William Doyle in the Lateran Basilica on Saturday 24 May 1755; both Irishmen received first Minor Orders and second Minor Orders from the same prelate in his private chapel on Sunday 29 June and Sunday 27 July, and on Saturday 20 September Sub-Diaconate

---

[2] England, *Life*, 224.

in the Lateran Basilica. After receiving Diaconate in the Patriarch's private chapel on Sunday 7 December Butler and Doyle were ordained during solemn mass in the Lateran Basilica by the vicegerent on the Saturday of Quarter Tense, 20 December 1755.[3]

Before returning home Fr Butler is believed to have taken his Doctorate of Divinity, after which he set about seeking a passage to Ireland. Having spent some time in Florence he came to Leghorn, but, as there was no vessel available there, he travelled to Marseilles, and then to Bordeaux before he found a ship sailing homeward. Even then he did not secure passage until the Duke of Richelieu, Governor of Bordeaux, intervened. The ship's captain reluctantly gave accommodation to four men, including the priest, on 17 October 1758, and sailed for Whitehaven, in Cumberland.

On docking there Capt. John Fletcher delivered the four over to a Justice of the Peace, who demanded depositions from them. That which Fr Butler submitted was preserved, and read as follows: "John Butler, of Grange, Ireland, Gentleman, now of the age of twenty-seven years. He was born at Grange, in the parish of Kiltinan. He is a single man and the third son of the late Lord Dunboyne of Grange, deceased. He is of no business or employment, never took the Oath of Allegiance to the king of France."[4]

Butler was not detained, and crossed over to Ireland. As priests did not wear any distinguishing dress at this period it was difficult for the port authorities to recognise them, even if they were anxious to detect clerics. So Fr Butler landed safely. As a new arrival from the continent, his news of the Seven Years War, and especially of his fellow countrymen fighting in either the English or foreign armies, would have been welcomed. He, in turn, would discover that in Dublin chapels prayers were requested for King George II, and that the monarch was assured Catholics would assist in obstructing any attempts at invasion by an alien power. In common with other prominent Catholics, Butler would appreciate the anomaly that caused his own brothers to serve in the French Army, although he and other clergymen swore to resist them if they arrived in the body of an invasion force. The Irish Parliament was strongly anti-Catholic; William of Orange was the Government's hero, and the strained relationship of that institution with the Crown was by then traditional. It was at this time immersed in seeking free trade and free legislation, in trying to control the vast pensions list, and in raising the taxes necessary to keep the ship of state afloat.

Back in his native diocese, now under the care of his cousin Archbishop James Butler I of Cashel, Fr Butler had to wait just a year for an appointment as parish priest of Ardmayle, in Co. Tipperary where he lodged with a family

---

[3] Archives of Vicariate of Rome, *Liber Ord.* 1754–1759, 95, 102, 108, 114, 128, 135.
[4] Burke, W.P., *Irish Priests in Penal Times*, 1914, 180.

named Strangs, at Cooleagh.[5] Fr Butler would have found conditions in the church more free than when he left Ireland. Except in times of war there was little persecution, and the king interfered in church affairs far less than Catholic rulers elsewhere. The chapels in which he administered would have been similar to that at Knockavella as described in Archbishop James Butler's Visitation book of 1759 "built by public collections; 14 couples and 2 ends, mud wall, well roofed and thatched: two windows with window sashes, not glazed, and one door. An altar of mud covered with a deal board".

The chapel at Knockgraffon in the same year was "a house about 60' long in the form of an L. Well thatched and kept, with a pretty good door well closed, and two pretty glazed windows, one at the side of a decent altar that is boarded at the front and a board step to it. A large picture of Xst upon the cross. A small brass crucifix . . . a casula stole maniple alb amict, two corporals, two purificatories bought by the parishioners; a small pewter chalice to be changed, and a borrowed Mass book".[6]

Additional appointments came the young priest's way; he was given the post of secretary to the archbishop, and made an archdeacon of the diocese.[7]

For the next four years Archdeacon Butler filled the role of rural parish priest, during which time he re-established his social position as one of the gentry. His friends would have included Protestants and Catholics of the landed class, and some years later, when the See of Cork became vacant, his relationship with the old established families proved useful.

Nine candidates were considered for the See, excluding Bishop Burke of Ossory, the proposed transfer of whom was seen by some authorities as the solution to a quarrel in which he was involved with one of his priests. Cardinal Spinelli, Prefect of Propaganda, informed the exiled Stuart king, James III, who still retained an interest in such nominations, of the various proposals.[8] The transfer of Bishop Burke was seen as difficult as it would involve incursion into a different province. It was recommended that someone from Cork would be more acceptable, "particularly the brother of Lord Dunboyne, an archdeacon and a parish priest in the province [of Munster], and he is recommended by his metropolitan".

In a list of the candidates, with their qualification, Cardinal Spinelli placed John Butler first. He was described as a former student of the Irish College and of Propaganda Fide, aged 33, a brother of Lord Dunboyne, and an archdeacon and parish priest of Ardmayle (modern parish of Dualla and Boherlahan) in the diocese of Cashel. Representations on his behalf had been made to the pope by the Archbishop of Cashel, the Bishop of Killaloe and the Bishop of Limerick.

---

5 *Rep. Novum*, John Kingston, iii, No. 1, 1961–2, 66.
6 CBACE, 52.
7 PBACE, 272.
8 A.P.F., S.C., Irlanda, Vol. XI, f. 251–6.

In a separate letter "this high personal quality and extremely noble blood" was stressed by his archbishop, these sentiments were echoed by Lord Taaffe, and by Edmond Butler, a brother to the Archbishop of Cashel. Cardinal Spinelli suggested that the diocese of Cork was in a bad state and the papal nuncio in Brussels supported him in seeking an early appointment from the recommended nine candidates.

The question of the Episcopal parish was also proving difficult. For generations the Coppinger family had the right of nomination to St. Mary's, which they had endowed. But now Cardinal Spinelli wrote that:

> ". . . with regard to the episcopal parish, I should not esteem it an advantage that the new bishop should obtain it from the pretended collator, but an infringement on the Holy See, whose rights could support a noble of the province against the pretender to the right of patronage. Wherefore I could not bring either my intelligence nor my conscience to acquiesce to the proposition."

On 16 April 1763, Archdeacon Butler was nominated by Pope Clement XIII as Bishop of Cork, and he was consecrated in June. He was but thirty-three years of age, and the Papal Brief commented on his youth that "he was barely the canonical age".[9]

A prolific local poet, Eadbhárd de Nógla, greeted the appointment with a

St. Patrick's Bridge, Cork, in the early 19th century

---

[9] *Hierarchia Catholica*, vi, 182. Padua 1958.

seven verse poem in the native language which, of course, would have been understood by the bishop. The poem offered "a thousand and one welcomes to this scion of Grecian blood, and faultless church leader . . . all Ireland rejoices at his coming". Nature, poets, mothers and children rejoiced, and considered the bishop "an ornament to his race, not come to oppress the poor". His paternal and maternal ancestry was praised; his father's hospitality and charity was seen as rewarded with the elevation of his son to the episcopacy. De Nógla concluded by regretting that, due to his advanced age, he was not able to do full justice to his subject, but he prayed that "Christ and Mary would be with John Butler".[10]

Less flattering was the opinion of a priest, Rev. T.R. England writing sixty years later: "the dignity of his birth, and the interest of some very powerful friends, led to his appointment . . . his learning was not extensive or profound . . .".[11]

Butler established himself in a country residence at Monkstown,[12] outside Cork, and he had a house at Pope's Quay in the city, where he was also parish priest of St Mary's parish. His church, popularly known as "the bishop's chapel", had been built in 1730 " . . . on a fine eminence, in a large sumptuous manner in the north suburbs, on a new foundation, near old St. Mary's Shandon churchyard". Bishop Butler's nomination to St Mary's does not seem to have had the traditional approval of the Coppingers, and over fifty years later members of that family were petitioning the pope for the resumption of their rights of nomination, a patronage which they had "enjoyed from time immemorial".[13] His status may have been similar to that of the next Metropolitan of Munster, as described by Margaret Gibbons in *Glimpses of Catholic Ireland*:

> "It was an age that worshipped rank as something sacrosanct; and Dr Butler's lineage from connections with the House of Ormonde opened doors that would have been closed contemptuously in the face of a mere titular bishop in those halcyon days of the Anglican Establishment in Ireland".[14]

---

[10] RIA, MS 24 M 30, 62-63. 1763. MS 23, 1, 26, 56. (See also M 8, 341, M 11, 220, St. Patrick's College, Maynooth).

[11] England, *Life*, 224.

[12] The late Eoin O'Mahony wrote the following to Lord Dunboyne on 5.4.1964: '[Bishop Butler] is believed to have lived in Monkstown on Cork Harbour when a bishop (where I was born). I like to think that it was in the late Elizabethan or early 17th century castle of the Goold's, still habitable and used now as a golf club. The bishop introduced into Cork diocese three priests whose parents were tenants or employees on the Dunboyne estate in Co. Tipperary. One was Fr. Prout PP of Watergrass hill who inspired Fr. Frank Mahony to write *Reliques* over that pseudonym. See also Cork Hist. Arch Jn. XLVIII, 1943, 26.

[13] A.P.F., S.Q. Irlanda, Vol. XXI, f. 102, f. 203-4, Vol. XXIII, f. 235. See also two undated Coppinger letters in the McCormack Papers in Franciscan Library, Killiney.

[14] Gibbons, *Glimpses*, 123.

If Bishop Butler was as well received as Miss Gibbons suggests it would have
been in marked contrast to the lifestyle of his cousin, the old Archbishop James
Butler I of Cashel. At one period he was said to have been "living in terror", [15]
and his letters were censored in an effort to incriminate the then Bishop of
Cork, believed to be a supporter of the pretender. When, at the end of his life
he lived openly in his diocese, the first prelate to do so since the Reformation,
his residence in Thurles was a thatched cabin, where he died in 1774. [16]

Bishop Butler held the See of Cork for twenty-three years. For the Catholics it was a period of gradual emergence from the Penal times into public
affairs. Charles O'Conor, of the ancient Irish Royal clan, had expressed the
loyalty of the people to the king, and the trust that the penal laws would be
removed. Liberal Protestants also sought relief for their Catholic neighbours,
and many of them went so far as to encourage the building of chapels by the
granting of sites.

In 1760 it was a Protestant, inspired by O'Conor, who in pleading for the
Catholics, gave this picture of his fellow-countrymen "they are lean and broken
hearted, even as a steer who lies abroad upon the windy heath, without cover-
ing or forage, throughout the winter. Four fifths of Irish Papists taste not bread
but as a dainty. Their habitation is no other than that of a few sods reared one
upon the other in the space of a few hours, and happy is that family who has the
milk of a single cow to kitchen a frugal parcel of sodden potatoes." [17]

The increase in agrarian outrages saw the introduction of the Coercion Act
in 1765; far from suppressing Whiteboyism, it forced the creation of further
secret societies, and multiplied the number of abuses. While the church, fearing
sectarian outrages, condemned these societies even to the extent of excommunicating members, it failed to daunt the agitators to any appreciable extent.
Bishop Butler, himself a member of the outraged class, denounced the Cork
Right-Boys, though he admitted that some of their grievances were not unrea-
sonable [18]

Twenty years later, in a pamphlet with the title "Loose thoughts on the
very important situation in Ireland, containing a distinction between the Catholics
and the Protestants", J. Williams commented:

> "I have seen twenty years ago, men with the uniform of French officers,
> disguised in white shirts, in the very act of disturbance amongst the White
> Boys . . . and knew at that time, that they were openly supported by the most
> powerful Catholics and titular bishops, who had cajoled government with
> their peaceable dispositions." [19]

---

[15] *Coll. Hib.*, Benignus Millet O.F.M., No. 1, 1958, 33.
[16] CBACE, 57.
[17] Gibbons, *Glimpses*, 47.
[18] Renehan, *Collections*, 346.
[19] Williams, J., *Loose thoughts . . . etc. on situation in Ireland*, 1785.

In Munster official action against the White Boys reached a peak on 15 March 1766 when the parish priest of Shandraghan, Ballysheehan, and Templeheney was hanged, drawn and quartered at Clonmel. Fr Nicholas Sheehy had already been acquitted of treason at the Court of King's Bench, in Dublin, when he was further charged with murder. He was taken to Clonmel by horse, with his legs tied beneath the animal's belly. Though there was evidence that the reputed victim had gone abroad the priest and another man were convicted on the evidence of disreputable witnesses, including that of a prostitute whom Fr Sheehy had denounced from the altar.

Although there was enormous public support for the priest, who was said to be an agitator and "inimical to tithe proctors and the oppressors of the poor", his bishop, Rt Rev. Dr Egan of Waterford and Lismore, refused to come forward to speak on his behalf. This prelate was believed to have been influenced by the Catholic aristocracy and the fear of further implications involving information against Dr James Butler I, Archbishop of Cashel. But the populace resented the inaction of Dr Egan, and when Sheehy's headless corpse was carried past his house, the priests blood was sprinkled on the bishop's door. The severed head of Fr Sheehy was displayed on a pole over Clonmel jail for almost twenty years, and would have been a familiar sight to John Butler, Bishop of Cork, whenever he had occasion to visit the town. The priest's grave soon became a place of pilgrimage, and when his skull was eventually given to his sister for burial a poem in Irish was composed to mark the event. Part of it, in translation, went like this:

> *Head of the martyr'd priest, I now can hold thee,*
> *Thus to my lips and to my heart I fold thee!*[20]

It was not long before a pamphlet on the execution was published in Cork; it held that Fr Sheehy learned of the murder of one John Bridges through the seal of the confessional, and the pamphlet was challengingly entitled "A parallel between the pretended plot in 1762 and the forgery of Titus Oates in 1679, being a sequel to the candid enquiry into the causes and motives of the late riots in the province of Munster".[21]

A grim sequel to Fr Sheehy's fate occurred four years later; while it demonstrated the long memory of the people, it also reflected the prevalent violence. On Thursday 6 September 1770 a murderer was being executed in Philipstown (now Daingean) and a huge crowd turned out for the event. As soon as the execution was over the mob turned on the hangman and stoned him to death,

---

[20] Sadlier, Mrs. J., *The Fate of Fr. Sheehy,* 1881.

[21] *A parallel between the plot in 1762 . . . and the forgery of Titus Oates in 1679,* Cork, 1767.

and for three days his body lay under the gallows. *Sleator's Public Gazetteer* of the 18 September, reporting the crime commented that "this unfortunate creature was the person who hung Sheehy the priest, which is supposed to be the reason for this outrage".[22] The city of Cork, at the time of Dr Butler's appointment to the See, was a thriving trading centre. Butter, pork and salt beef were packed and exported through the port which was described as the "busiest, most animated scene of shipping in all Ireland". Despite the usual entertainments such as balls, theatre, whist and concerts, the well stocked book shops and the publication of local papers, a French visitor in 1797 found the city "very gloomy and dirty, you are every moment stopped by funerals, droves of cattle, or beggars, who go through the streets by dozens, and yet this city is one of the richest and most commercial in Europe".[23] Some twenty years earlier Rev. John Wesley had preached in the city. His subject was "[t]o abstain from fleshly desires" which, he said, "was a necessary lesson in every place and nowhere more so than in Cork".[24] Evidence of a good standard of printing there can be found in two little ecclesiastical publications from the press of one Eugene Swiney; dated 1764 and 1768 respectively[25] the *Apparatus ad Clericorum Institutionem* and the *Statuta Synodalia pro Diaecesi Corcagiensi* must both have been issued at the behest of Dr Butler, though neither bears his *imprimatur*.

The first is a primer for the education of clerics prior to examination for orders, and the second outlines the Statutes for the diocese relating to faith, the nature of the priestly life, the mass, the parish and preaching. The preacher was advised not to talk over the heads of his flock, to avoid levity, apocryphal stories, inauthentic miracles and the prediction of future events; it recommended that he should prepare himself with knowledge derived from study and meditation. The Statutes also listed the reserved sins, among which were association with the Whiteboys, taking part in Protestant worship, heresy, apostasy, and clerics having or attempting carnal copulation.

When Bishop Butler issued the Statutes listing the reserved sins in 1768 he may have been mindful of a scandal in the neighbouring diocese of Cloyne and Ross which his metropolitan had asked him to investigate a couple of years before. There was bad feeling between Archbishop James Butler I of Cashel and Bishop John O'Brien of Cloyne and Ross for almost twenty years. On his succession to the See of Cloyne and Ross in 1748 Dr O'Brien did not renew Butler's appointment as vicar general, and he much resented that Butler should hold the important parish of Mitchelstown, as well as that of neighbouring Kilbeheny in Emly diocese. After Dr Butler's elevation as coadjutor to the

---

[22] Brady, *18th c. Press*, 140. For another version of this story see *The Celt*, 1857.

[23] La Tocnaye, Le. Chev. de, *Rambles through Ireland*, Cork. 1798, i, 123.

[24] *Journal of the Rev. John Wesley, A.M.* iv, n.d., 122.

[25] *Apparatus ad Clericorum Institutionem*, 1764, and *Statuta Synodalia pro Diaecesi Corcagiensi*, 1768. E. Swiney, Cork.

John Butler OF CORK.

The bookplate of John Butler, Bishop of Cork

archbishop in 1750 he was permitted to keep Mitchelstown parish, much to the annoyance of Dr O'Brien. His efforts to have Butler removed from Mitchelstown failed, and when in 1757 Butler was nominated Archbishop of Cashel and still retained the parish, Dr O'Brien protested to Rome.[26] A year later he took the extraordinary step of excommunicating the inhabitants of the town, and amongst the priests who expounded this censure to his flock, was Fr Nicholas Sheehy, described as "an unregistered priest". Lord Kingston, the local landlord, was much incensed by this edict, as it adversely affected the trade of the town, and he retaliated by putting an award of twenty pounds on the head of the bishop and five pounds on the heads of the supporting clergy.[27]

Now, in 1766, there was further aggravation between Archbishop James I and Dr O'Brien of Cloyne and Ross. For some twenty years the parish priest of Clondrohid, in Dr O'Brien's diocese, had kept a concubine. The bishop had succeeded a few years before in separating Fr Florence MacCarthy from this woman; but on visiting Clondrohid in 1766 ". . . during the general mission, when I spent four or five days in the parish with sixteen of my best missionaries, I discovered that MacCarthy had begun again to live with this married woman".[28] The bishop used the strong hand, and at a general assembly of all the parishioners suspended the parish priest "for his public crimes".

---

[26] CBACE, 230 *et seq.*

[27] Brady, *18th c. Press,* 94-5, 105.

[28] Letter from Bishop of Cloyne & Ross to Cardinal Castelli dated 25 Nov. 1766 in documents *Fondo Missioni* of the Vatican Archives.

---

[29] Letter from Bishop of Cloyne & Ross to Cardinal Castelli dated 25 Nov. 1766 in

Dr O'Brien informed his archbishop, and was very annoyed when he commissioned the bishop of Cork, "his own relation", to decide the case. Dr O'Brien sent a bitter letter of complaint to Cardinal Castelli, Prefect of Propaganda, begging help ". . . in a case of extreme necessity. Unless Propaganda revokes the [Bishop of Cork's] commission, all of my work of visitation and correction will be rendered useless".[29]

Bishop John Butler wrote to Cloyne and Ross about the case on 10 December. He warned Dr O'Brien that if Fr MacCarthy was not permitted to appeal the sentence to his metropolitan by noon of the following day that he would pronounce in favour of MacCarthy, and transmit his findings to Rome "where, no doubt, they will be approved".[30] Twelve days later Dr Butler again wrote to Dr O'Brien that he objected to his practice of denying his priests right of appeal to their metropolitan, "for this reason and no other, I have just passed favourable sentence, even against my own better judgement, on Fr MacCarthy".[31]

This decision greatly displeased Dr O'Brien, and he wrote a strong letter of complaint to the papal nuncio at Brussels. The Bishop of Cork's decision, he suggested, was inspired by his ambition to become coadjutor of Cashel. Could a bishop, he asked, who would pronounce sentence against his own judgement, be capable of anything natural, good or proper? He described his own visitations to Clondrohid, but now, as he was in poor health, he must go to the Spa near Liege, and leave his Will with his administrators.[32]

In May, however, he was still in his diocese, and again complaining to Rome about the Archbishop of Cashel. He pointed out that he himself followed the Council of Trent, unlike the other three priests, Cashel, Cork and MacCarthy. He enclosed a list of Fr MacCarthy's crimes, and said that if propaganda should decide in favour of Cashel that his authority within Cloyne and Ross would be nil, and the fruits of his mission lost.[33] Thus the controversy between the metropolitan and Dr O'Brien continued, possibly with faults on both sides. One commentator has remarked that throughout the affair Dr O'Brien's letters "were couched in very violent and intemperate language", and

---

documents *Fondo Missioni* of the Vatican Archives.

[30] CBACE, 233.

[31] AP.F., S.C., Irlanda, Vol. XI, f. 342: Letter from Bishop of Cork to Bishop of Cloyne & Ross dated Cork 22 Dec. 1766 in documents *Fondo Missioni* of the Vatican Archives.

[32] Undated letter from bishop of Cloyne & Ross to papal nuncio at Brussels in documents *Fondo Missioni* of the Vatican Archives.

[33] Letter from bishop of Cloyne & Ross to Cardinal Castelli dated 30 May 1767 in documents *Fondo Missioni* of the Vatican Archives.

[34] CBACE, 233-4.

*Part of a candelabrum which was hung in the South Chapel, Cork in 1770 to
commemorate the foundation of a Sodality of the Blessed Virgin by Bishop Butler 'of
the Barons Dunboyne'*

that "Archbishop Butler's relations with a considerable number of his clergy
were not entirely happy". [34]

The feuding ended with the death of the bishop of Cloyne and Ross at
Cambrai in the spring of 1769.[35] Dr Butler continued in Cashel until he died,
aged 83, in 1774. The fate of Fr Florence MacCarthy is not known, but his
circumstances must have sometimes crossed the mind of his protector, the Bishop
of Cork.

Within a decade of Butler's succession to the Cork diocese three chapels
were built, bringing the total in the city to eight, apart from "many private
places of worship where friaries are held".[36] The new churches were St Finbarr's
or South Chapel, and those at Minane Bridge and at Ballymartle. The first

---

[35] Brady, *18th c. Press,* 134.
[36] *Freeman's Journal,* 18 February 1772.

mentioned replaced an older one which had collapsed, and the new building was undertaken by the parish priest, Fr Daniel O'Brien O.P., V.G., in 1766. It was L-shaped, with a "so called women's isle".[37] Bishop Butler would have blessed this and the other churches. It remains in Dunbar Street, much altered since 1805, as a memorial of his reign. Another reminder of that period has been found. It is part of an elaborate twelve-branched brass candelabrum which was hung in the sanctuary of the South Chapel in 1770. An inscription in Latin records that it was installed to mark the foundation of the Sodality of the B.V.M. four years before by Bishop Butler "of the Barons Dunboyne".[38] City gossip suggested that "swarms of Jesuits" were being imported daily into Cork, and that nuns, brought from the continent, were about to seduce and make converts of Protestant children. Despite his prejudice, the Protestant who included these charges in his letter to the *Freeman's Journal,* dated 1 February 1772, unwittingly recorded an important impression of the emergence of Catholic life in Cork at that time. The letter writer saw everywhere the hidden hand of Rome, endeavouring to "overturn our once happy constitution". His melancholy conclusion was that if the Act, to allow Papists to take long leases of property, was passed "you will not in a few years hence hear in this town the name of a Protestant". He may also have been perturbed at the findings of the 1766 census of Protestants and Catholics in the country. The returns were made by the clergy of the Church of Ireland on a parish basis and, for example, that of the parish of Dun Bolg, near Cork city, showed seven Protestant families, containing 20 persons, and 306 Catholic families, containing 1,662 persons. There was "no resident Popish priest or Fryar in the parish of Dunbulluck, but he who attends as such is Danl. McCarthy".[39]

This alarmed gentleman did find some small consolation in a recent occurrence in the city. A public theological disputation on the consistency of the Roman and Protestant faiths was arranged for one of the chapels; Bishop Butler himself undertook to represent Rome, while Fr Joseph Halloran S.J., "a gentleman of the tribe of Loyola", supported the Established Church. The discussion lasted for several days, with the bishop entirely refuting the Protestant arguments, much to the satisfaction of the audience who "testified their joy by repeated shouts". An aspect of the dialogue which infuriated the correspondent to the Dublin newspaper was that while this "public insult to the laws" was

---

[37] Walsh, T.J., *In the tradition of St. Finbarr,* 1951.
[38] Later it was removed to Bantry parish church where it hung in the central porch. From there it was taken to Messrs. Egan's of Cork. Mr. P. O'Keeffe, Bantry, located the remaining parts of the candelabrum and through Ms. Patricia Hutchins presented them to The Butler Society in 1977. It was acquired for St. Patrick's College, Maynooth in 1978. Also in the College is a sideboard which Dunboyne is believed to have used as an altar on which to say Mass after his marriage.
[39] *Cork Hist. Arch Jn.* 11, 1946, 69–77.

known to everyone in Cork, no champion raised his head "to assist the *good natured* Jesuit", either from the magistrates or clergy. The only support the priest got was from a cooper who, "with more zeal than wit", opposed the bishop "to his great confusion and dismay". While the cooper may have triumphed in church, he lost in the street; it would seem that his temerity incurred the anger of his fellow citizens, and he was driven to beggary and ruin.[40]

Nor did the Jesuit, Fr Halloran, escape the law. On 29 March 1772 bills of indictment were issued by the Cork city Grand Jury against him for "endeavouring to pervert some of his majesty's Protestant subjects, and persuading them to embrace the erroneous doctrines of Popery etc." In the same report *Faulkner's Dublin Journal* of 9 April identified the priest as "the person that had the daring insolence, together with the titular Bishop, publicly in a Popish chapel near Shandon church, to set at defiance the laws of the realm, by reflecting on and attempting to overthrow the fundamentals of the Established Church, and in contempt of the indulgence given to Papists by our mild and gracious government".

Other events in the city early in that year of 1772 explain why a cooper had the audacity to rise in the "Popish chapel near Shandon church" and contradict Bishop Butler.[41] On 2 January the "Distressed Journeymen Weavers" protested in the *Cork Hibernian Chronicle* that their trade was experiencing a severe slump due to the public not having their clothing lined and trimmed as formerly. The weavers pleaded for a return to the old style. Then, a couple of weeks later, a wool-draper's shop was attacked as it "sold English and Dublin goods with its own manufacture". A few days later a linen-draper's premises in Tuckey's St was raided by a mob accompanied by three revenue officers, in search of smuggled goods. Cars coming into the city were attacked and goods examined. The coopers, following the example of the weavers, began to show signs of dissatisfaction and "combined together to enter into giddy and detestable resolutions, tending to the prejudice, if not the total ruin of the trade of this city".

Bishop Butler penned a strong "Exhortation" on the disorders, and had it read in all chapels in the city. No doubt, but it was a cooper inflamed by the pastoral, who took issue, when the opportunity arose, with his bishop. This was the text of the "Exhortation", as printed in the *Cork Hibernian Chronicle* on 10 February:

> "It is with deepest concern, dearly beloved Brethren, we observe that a riotous spirit has of late manifested itself amongst some orders of journeymen tradesmen of this city, who in open defiance of all laws divine and human, and in contempt of lawful authority, have dared to assemble in numerous

[40] Brady, *18th c. Press*, 148–9.
[41] I am indebted to the late Mr. Sean Daly, Tower Books, Cork, for this reference.

bodies, and march in such a tumultuous manner through the city, for their wicked and audacious purposes, as to alarm the peaceable good inhabitants thereof, who could not but apprehend the worst consequences from a mob so infatuated and ill-disposed as to commit, under the most shameful and absurd pretext, the most heinous excesses and robberies, in cutting, burning, spoiling and carrying off the goods, wares and merchandise of their fellow subjects and fellow citizens on the public roads, and even in their houses, which they forcibly entered. And whereas the journey- men coopers viewing the impunity with which the journey-men weavers assembled and carried on their villainous proceeding, have from the same evil spirit of riot and disorder combined together to enter into giddy and detestable resolutions, rending to the prejudice, if not to the total ruin of the trade of this city, consequently to the utter ruin of themselves, their wives and children, and have taken on themselves to print and publish the same, coaching them in terms so dictatorial and absolute as nothing but their presumptuous insolence and folly can account for.

Now, in order to put a stop, as far as in us lies, to such enormities and excesses, we do hereby, in the name of Almighty God, in our quality of Pastors, strictly charge and command all such of our flock, as deluded by the artifices of the Devil, might have joined, aided or abetted such dangerous and illegal proceedings, to make all possible atonement and satisfaction to the injured public, by a most exemplary, quiet, and peaceable behaviour, and an inviolable, veneration for the laws in future; to restore to the honest proprietors all such goods, wares and merchandise as they have stolen; to make full and ample restitution, as far as they are, in any sort, able, to all such as have suffered by the spoiling, burning, cutting or destroying their goods; all which we enjoin them to the performance of as they tender their eternal salvation; and further, to separate themselves from all such as may be wicked enough to continue depredations and combinations, so destructive to their own and their families good, so obnoxious to the public peace, and so subversive of the prosperity of the trade of this city, declaring at the same time, that, should any of our flock and communion, be found, notwithstanding our earnest exhortations and injunctions, to join in, or enter into any such outrageous and illegal acts or confederacies, they shall be looked upon as rebellious children, as rotten Members unworthy our Communion; and as such, shall be publicly denounced excommunicated, from all the altars in our places of public worship. But no, obedient to the voice of religion and reason, penetrated with a hearty detestation of past excesses, we hope to see them give to their fellow tradesmen and citizens of every other profession or denomination, the example of perfect obedience to the laws of the land, and to submission to the rulers that God has placed over them; and should the Lord think proper to chastise them for their sins by a stagnation in the different branches of their respective trades, and the miseries that commonly attend the like, instead of flying in the face of providence, as they have, heretofore, by joining in combinations, linked together by the most execrable oaths and supported by drunkenness and debauchery, they will kiss the paternal hand that strikes them for their good, and suffer with Christian patience and resignation the trials they are visited with; thus they will appease the wrath of God, satisfy his injured justice, and instead of those curses they entail on themselves and their families, by their criminal excesses they will draw down blessings from Heaven, and merit a share hereafter in the Kingdom of eternal glory which God has promised to the righteous, and to all that suffer in this life for justice sake. Amen."

Alas, the tradesmen did not heed their pastor, and the *Cork Hibernian Chronicle* of 2 July reported a dispute about rates between journey-men carpenters and "some carpenters who style themselves Masters".

Although public discussion of religion was not uncommon in those times, it is interesting to find Dr Butler involved in disputing the merits of the two national faiths. When his brother Pierce, an officer in the French army, had inherited the Dunboyne title four years before, he abandoned Rome for the Established Church,[42] but the relationship between the bishop and his apostate brother does not seem to have deteriorated as a result. Nor did the accounts of Bishop Butler's later years show him as a champion of much ardour. While the Penal Laws may appear to have been ignored, it is sobering to see that a month before this debate, and again in February 1772, men in Cork city were being gaoled for carrying or concealing firearms, "being Papists".[43]

In an effort to dispel the belief of Protestants that Catholics could not be loyal subjects, the Catholic bishops and prominent laymen endeavoured to establish their loyalty by every means. At last, by the 1774 Act 13 and 14 George III, c. 35, they were given an explicit formula by which they could declare themselves. This was the form of the new Oath of Allegiance, which contained the substance of the Oaths of Abjuration and Supremacy, and was to be taken before a magistrate or justice of the peace:

> "I, A.B., do take almighty God and His only son Jesus Christ my Redeemer to witness, that I will be faithful and bear true allegiance to our most gracious sovereign lord, King George the Third, and him will defend to the utmost of my power against all conspiracies and attempts whatever, that shall be made against his person, crown and dignity; and I will do my utmost endeavour to disclose and make known to his majesty, and his heirs, all treasons and traitorous conspiracies which may be formed against him or them; and I do faithfully promise to maintain, support and defend, to the utmost of my power, the succession of the crown in his majesty's family, against any person or persons whatsoever, hereby utterly renouncing and abjuring any obedience or allegiance unto the person taking upon himself the stile and title of Prince of Wales, in the lifetime of his father, and who since his death is said to have assumed the stile and title of King of Great Britain and Ireland, by the name

---

[42] Finegan, Francis S.J., *Studies*, XXXVIII, 1949, 79. Healy, *Maynooth*, 296.
[43] Brady, *18th c. Press*, 148–9.

of Charles the Third, and to any other person claiming or pretending a right
to the crown of these realms; and I do swear that I do reject and detest as
unchristian and impious to believe, that it is lawful to murder or destroy any
person or persons whatsoever, for or under pretence of their being heretics;
and I further declare, that it is no article of my faith, and that I do renounce,
reject and abjure the opinion, that princes excommunicated by the pope and
council, or by any authority of the See of Rome, or by any authority
whatsoever, may be deposed or murdered by their subjects, or by any person
whatsoever; and I do promise that I will not hold, maintain, or abet, any such
opinion, or any other opinion, contrary to what is expressed in this declaration;
and I do declare, that I do not believe, that the Pope of Rome or any other
foreign prince, prelate, state or potentate hath, or ought to have any temporal
or civil jurisdiction, power, superiority or pre-eminence, directly or indirectly,
within this realm; and I do solemnly in the presence of God, and of His only
Son Jesus Christ, my Redeemer, profess, testify and declare, that I do make
this declaration and every part thereof, in the plain and ordinary sense of the
words of this Oath, without any evasion, equivocation, or mental reservation
whatsoever, and without any dispensation already granted by the pope or any
authority of the See of Rome, or any person whatsoever; and without thinking
that I am or can be acquitted before God or man, or absolved of this declaration,
or any part thereof, although the pope, or any other person or persons, or
authority whatsoever shall dispense with or annul the same or declare that it
was null and void from the beginning. So help me God."

The formula was not, however, acceptable to all of the Catholic hierarchy, and
its proposed adoption caused a serious division in the ranks. The opinion of the
professors of the University of Paris was sought, and 150 of them agreed that
the Oath could be taken.[44] At a session presided over by the newly-appointed
Archbishop James Butler II of Cashel it was decided that the Oath, though
objectionable and harsh, "contained nothing positively contrary to the princi-
ples of the Catholic religion". This decision, dated Cork 15 July 1775, was
signed by Dr James Butler II and six suffragans, including the Bishop of Cork.[45]
Other prelates considered the Oath as a declaration by which "the Irish were to
be Catholics first and British subjects afterwards, or vice versa",[46] and the Archbishops of Tuam and Dublin, with several bishops, believed the Oath to be
unlawful.[47] The Cork capuchin, Fr Arthur O'Leary, published a tract entitled
"Loyalty asserted, or the Test Oath Vindicated, in a Letter to a Protestant Gentleman", as he held that it was strictly compatible with the tenets of the church.
    This liberalism on the part of the southern clergy was seen as a reflection of
their French education, where theologians were fond of "exaggerating the civil

---

[44] CBACE, 125.
[45] CBACE, 126.
[46] Gibbons, *Glimpses,* 120.
[47] Ibid., 123.

power of the State, at the expense of the ecclesiastical power of the pope".[48]
Some commentators saw the issue as a British plot to create a schism in the Irish
church.[49] In 1772 Bishop Burke of Ossory, a Dominican, published a supple-
ment to his *Hibernia Dominicana,* and included a copy of a letter from an apostolic
nuncio which emphatically insisted that Catholics could not subscribe to an
earlier version of the Test Oath. Now, five days after approving of the 1774
Oath, the Archbishop of Cashel and the same six bishops condemned Burke's
publication, because it might weaken allegiance to the king.[50]

During the month of December 1775 the first of the bishops to take the
Oath, Dr James Keeffe of Kildare and Leighlin, did so on 4 December. He was
soon followed by many others, including the Archbishop of Cashel. He subscribed to the formula, according to *Faulkner's Dublin Journal,* on Friday 15
December in Thurles. Many of the diocesan clergy, and several "respectable
Roman Catholic gentlemen, merchants and trading inhabitants of the town"
were sworn at the same time. After Christmas Dr Butler II, received this letter
from the Bishop of Cork:

> "I would be earlier in wishing Your Grace every happiness, but I was so busy.
> The same excuse will serve for my not appearing before a magistrate to take
> the test. I could not come sooner to town, and the weather was so bad, and
> my clergy so busy, that I could not call them together to accompany me. I
> shall as soon as ever I can go about it. I fear the friars of this town will take
> advantage of it to hurt me in the eyes of those they influence in this town,
> which are not a small number . . . But if religion gains by it, I don't care. I fear
> the troubles at home and abroad will prevent parliament or administration
> from attempting anything at present. . . ."[51]

Perhaps John Butler of Cork was being more prudent than his superior and his
fellow bishops, as in the summer following his subscription to the Oath the
Archbishop of Cashel was in communication with Propaganda in Rome on the
subject. While he insisted that the oath was acceptable, he was told to restrain
himself, and that he should have consulted Rome before he acted.[52] So this
matter dragged on, and in 1777 the archbishop was still vindicating his position
to Rome, explaining that Munster, due to outbreaks of Whiteboyism, was in a
special position.[53] Now the See of Ossory was vacant, but the new appointee
was to be another Dominican, Dr Troy, that he too would be opposed to the

---

[48] Gibbons, *Glimpses,* 123.

[49] Ibid., 121.

[50] CBACE, 126.

[51] Power, T.R., *Irish Ecclesiastical Record,* 1892, XIII, 302–318; 522–538; 1893, XIV,
275–283.

[52] CBACE, 132–3.

[53] CBACE, 134.

Test Oath, Dr Butler II was warned by his sister Mary.[54] The controversy
continued, and it was not until the passing of the Catholic Relief Bill in August
1778, that the matter terminated. In that year the Bishop of Cork took the Test
Oath, at Clonmel Assizes; he was but one of the 487 persons in Co. Tipperary
who subscribed to the oath between 1775 and 1787, for which period the returns are recorded.[55] This is how the *Dublin Evening Post* noted the event in its
edition of 6 October 1778:

> "Cork, Oct. 1. Tuesday the Hon. and Rt. Rev. Dr. John Butler, titular Bishop
> of this diocese, and a great number of the Roman Catholic clergy belonging
> to this diocese and Cloyne, took and subscribed the Oath of Allegiance be-
> fore the judges of assize; as did also above seven hundred reputable Roman
> Catholic ladies and gentlemen residing in this city and county, and in the
> counties adjacent."

Some progress towards a better status for Catholics was achieved in 1778 with
the Act which enabled them to hold leases for nine hundred and ninety-nine
years, and to devise and transfer lands. While throughout the body of the Bill
the Catholics were described as Papists, or persons professing the Popish religion, in the preamble the term Roman Catholics of Ireland was used.

Richard Mant, historian of the Established Church, noted that, "at about
this period it appears that the professors of the Romish religion were unlawfully
attributing to their rulers distinctions which belonged lawfully only to rulers of
the Irish church".[56] Catholic bishops were referred to in government statutes
and proclamations, and in the press, as titular because legally they did not exist.
According to the law, and until the dis-establishment of the church in 1869, the
only bishops recognised by the law were those of the Established Church. Showing his customary punctiliousness the Archbishop of Cashel, Dr James Butler II,
writing in 1777 referred to his fellow prelates as titular and as "chiefs of the
Roman Catholic religion", which indicated his respect for authority.[57] The
man in the street was not unduly influenced by such formality and when a
visitor to Cork, on leaving the Protestant Cathedral in 1778, asked to be directed to the bishop's house he was asked: "Which bishop?"[58]

It was in that year also that the Butlers of Ormonde suffered a scandal when
the thirty-nine year-old daughter of the *de jure* 16th Earl, a Catholic, eloped
with a young Ponsonby girl. Eleanor Butler was a grand-niece of the late Archbishop Christopher Butler of Cashel, a man much persecuted during his

---

[54] CBACE, 135.
[55] *Journal of the House of Commons*, CXXVIII, 6 February 1792.
[56] Mant, R., *History of the Established Church*, 1840, ii, 609.
[57] Morris, Thomas, *North Munster Antiquarian Journal*, 1955, vii, No. 2, 13, 23.
[58] Gibbons, *Glimpses*, 130.

episcopacy (1712-1757). Madame Butler hoped that her ageing daughter would enter a nunnery in Cambrai, an intention not shared by Sarah Ponsonby who was determined to "do anything to save Miss Butler from Popery and a Convent". She succeeded, and both women retired to the seclusion of a Welsh valley where they regularly attended a Reformed Church, and lived happily together for fifty years. However, it is unlikely that the Kilkenny scandal unduly worried the archbishop or the bishop as they had already seen Eleanor's brother John renouncing Catholicism in 1764 when he was endeavouring to reverse the attainder on the family titles.[59] Both prelates would, by this, be unhappily familiar with instances of perversion. In the year that Dr Butler succeeded to the See of Cork several of his flock were reported in the newspapers as recanting "from the errors of Rome", including Miss Mary Twomey of Scull at St. Nicholas's Church in Cork.[60] The certificate which she signed would have been similar to that completed by another Mary, also in Cork fourteen years before. Miss Mary Murphy had been received into the Communion of the Church of Ireland on 20 August 1749, as she had subscribed to this document a week before:

> "Having from my Childhood been brought up in the Communion of the Church of Rome, I account it a great Blessing, that I have had the Opportunity of discovering the Errors of that Profession, in which I have so long lived; and in which if I should continue, I am very sensible that I should highly displease Almighty God.
>
> For the discharging therefore of my own conscience, as well as the satisfaction of all good Christians, I here make profession of that Faith and Religion in and by which I hope to be saved; and also renounce and disclaim those Errors and Corruptions which I take to be destructive of Salvation.
>
> I receive the Holy Scriptures, as containing the whole revealed Will and Law of God; neither do I own the belief or practice of any thing to be necessary to Salvation, except it be either therein read, or may be proved thereby.
>
> I believe in God the Father Almighty, Maker of Heaven and Earth: and in Jesus Christ his only Son our Lord, who was conceived by the Holy Ghost, born of the Virgin Mary, suffered under Pontius Pilate, was crucified, dead and buried, he descended into Hell; the third Day he rose again from the dead, he ascended into Heaven, and sitteth on the right Hand of God the Father Almighty; from thence he shall come to judge the quick and the dead.
>
> I believe in the Holy Ghost; the Holy Catholic Church; the Communion of Saints; the Forgiveness of Sins; the Resurrection of the Body; and the Life everlasting. Amen.

---

[59] Mavor, Elizabeth, *The Ladies of Llangollen,* 1971, 41.
[60] Brady, *18th c. Press,* 107.

And whosoever believes and professes this Faith, and, having been by Baptism admitted into the Church of Christ, leads his Life according to the Gospel of Christ, I am fully persuaded will be accepted of God, and if he continues in the same good course to the end of his life, will certainly be saved.

I believe that all religious Worship is to be paid to God alone; and therefore do resolve for the Time to come, not to give any religious Worship of any kind, nor to offer up Prayers or Devotions to the Virgin Mary, or to any Saint, Angel, or Image whatsoever.

I faithfully promise through the Grace of God, to lead an holy life in the constant practice of my whole duty to God, to my self, and to all other men, and to the best of my Power to abstain from all sin and wickedness, in thought, word and deed.

I hope for Pardon of my Sins from the Mercy of God, through the Merits, Death, and sufferings of Jesus Christ; neither do I hold or depend upon any other Merits or Sacrifice for Sin but his alone, who offered himself once upon the Cross, as a sacrifice or ransom for the sins of the world. And therefore I reject the pretended sacrifice of the Mass, together with all the pretended Merits of the Saints, and Works of Superogation, as mere groundless and corrupt inventions.

I believe that God alone can forgive Sins; and that the condition on which alone God has promised pardon of sins through Jesus Christ, is sincere repentance, and Amendment to Life: All those practices therefore of the Church of Rome, of Confession to the Priest, Absolution, Indulgences, Penance, Pilgrimages, or other bodily Mortifications, as they are no where commanded or warranted in the Holy Scriptures, I look upon to be in themselves ineffectual to this end, and to be calculated to delude Men by false Hopes of Pardon of Sins without quitting and forsaking them.

I believe that all Christians who live in the Faith and Fear of God, shall be for ever happy in Heaven; and that they who live wickedly and die in their sins, shall be for ever miserable in Hell. But as for the Romish Doctrine of Purgatory, together with their practice of saying Masses, and granting Indulgences for the delivery of Souls from thence, I look upon them to be all vain and groundless, and therefore do utterly disclaim and reject them.

I promise to frequent the public Worship of God, as it is performed in the Church of Ireland; the Form of which I look upon to be decent and proper, and agreeable to the Commands of God; particularly in this, that all the Prayers and other public Offices are in a Language understood by the people.

I believe it to be the duty of all Christians, frequently to partake of the holy communion of the Body and Blood of Christ, according to his holy institution, in remembrance of his Death and Passion. But the Romish Doctrine of Transubstantiation, together with their Practice of worshipping the Host, (as they call it) and frequently carrying it about in procession for that purpose, as also that of denying the Cup to the Laity, I utterly reject and disavow, as being not only void of all foundation in Holy Scripture, but in a great measure contrary thereto, as well as to right reason and my own senses.

I acknowledge that proper Honour ought to be paid to the lawful Ministers, Pastors and Governors of the Church of Christ: But the Doctrines of Supremacy of the Pope and Bishop of Rome, of his being the Vicar of Christ, and Head upon Earth of the universal Church; or that either he, or the Church in Communion with him, are infallible in Matters of Faith, all these Doctrines, together with their Consequences, I reject as unsound, and built upon no foundation in the Holy Scriptures.

I earnestly beg of God, and desire all good Christians to do the same for me, that he would be pleased to strengthen and confirm me in the belief of what I now profess, and enable me by his Grace to lead the remainder of my life according thereunto; granting me true repentance and pardon for all my errors and sins past, and guiding and conducting me for the time to come in the Way of his holy Laws and Commandments.

In which course that I may continue unto my Life's end, and thereby become partaker of eternal happiness through Jesus Christ our Lord, I earnestly desire to be admitted into the Communion and Fellowship of the Church of Ireland, as now it stands by Law established." [61]

While the offensive wording of the Renunciation formula was probably well known to the Catholic clergy, they themselves, when an opportunity arose, could be equally explicit about the errors of Protestantism. And in many instances they must have known that the recanters were motivated more by material than spiritual gain. Furthermore, the re-emergence of their own people from the days of darkness meant that they were kept occupied with many practical as well as theological problems.

Catholic schools were being re-established throughout the country, and a small community of Discalced Carmelite Nuns were in Cork since 1742. The pioneering Nano Nagle, founder of the Presentation Order, maintained seven schools in Cork from 1755. While the bishop welcomed these endeavours, he was not always as prompt in co-operating with the ladies as they expected that he might be. Miss Nagle later engaged in bringing the Ursuline Sisters to the city, but the bishop felt that she might first have sought the consent of the Protestant ascendancy, an opinion which she did not share. [62] Generally, the relationship between the sisters and the Ordinary was good, and on one occasion when a postulant left the Presentation convent and joined the Ursulines the bishop was asked to intervene, and he directed, and both communities agreed, that one order would not accept subjects rejected by the other. [63] Fr

---

[61] TCD MS. 378.
[62] Walsh, *Nagle*, 69.
[63] Walsh, *Nagle*, 111.

Lawrence Callanan O.F.M, of whom the bishop approved, was Spiritual Director to Miss Nagle.[64]

The Ursulines had been established in the city in 1771 when, to quote from the *Annals* of that House, "Mass was celebrated for the first time in the chapel of the monastery and the Most Blessed Sacrament solemnly deposited in the Tabernacle by His Lordship, the Right Reverend Dr. John Butler". During the following sixteen years the bishop regularly officiated at convent ceremonies, the Reception and Profession of novices and triennial visitations, thus fulfilling the obligation vested in him by Pope Clement XIV in 1773. The Papal Brief gave the new foundation the same "indulgences and privileges conferred on the Parisian Monastery", on which establishment's plan the Cork house was based. The Brief included a phrase which indicated that the episcopal work of Dr Butler was not unknown in Rome, as the Secretary of the Congregation of the Propagation of the Faith brought to the Holy Father's notice "in his usual pleasing and accurate manner . . . many good things of your [Butler's] pastoral solicitude in your apostolical functions".[65]

The Augustinian friars, who had been in Cork since the 14th century, had survived the worst rigours of the penal times. By 1769 the community consisted of only four men, but the provincial hoped that Dr Butler would permit them to open a noviciate in the city.[66]

At this period the status of the various orders of friars was disputed, and since 1751 the bishops could appoint them to parishes, if necessary. Some of the secular clergy believed that the total disbandment of the religious might be desirable, and while Dominicans, Franciscans and Discalced Carmelites also had houses in the diocese, the bishop did not permit them to open noviciates. Or, as one commentator has remarked, the friars "may not have made a formal request lest it should weaken even more their already strained relations with the bishop".[67] The Dominican provincial abandoned the idea of a noviciate there in 1774.[68]

There is further evidence of an unhappy relationship between the ordinary and the regular clergy of the diocese.[69] For fourteen years, a Dominican, who was also prior of the local community, held the post of parish priest of the chapel of St Finbarr in Dunbar St. In 1774 he was succeeded by the Cork born

---

[64] Mooney, Canice, OFM, *Franciscan Cork*, N.D., 19. Brennan, M.J. OSF, *Life of V.Rev. L Callanan,* 1818, 26.

[65] AUCC, i.

[66] Fenning, *Undoing*, 301.

[67] Ibid., 322.

[68] Ibid., 320.

[69] A.P.F., S.C.Irlanda, vol. 12, f. 121-2, 205 *et seq.*

secular priest Fr Francis Moylan, who had been educated in Toulouse, and who would later transfer from the See of Kerry to Cork. The appointment of Fr Moylan was not popular with the regular clergy, as can be seen from this letter to Fr Charles O'Kelly OP, in Rome dated 27 March 1774.[70] The writer was a Dominican who, apart from a short period in Rome, had spent most of his life in Cork and had been prior to his community for a time. The letter read:

"Very Rev. Fr. Master,

The many and repeated uneasiness given us by his Lordship Dr. John Butler occasion us to trouble you so often, but he lately told his mind to Mr. French, Provincial of the Franciscans, by which he gives us the finishing stroke. He assured him that he wrote to Rome to get leave to remove the regular clergy from officiating in their respective chapels and to officiate daily in the two parish chapels of this city, and solicited for several other favours if that did not take place, all to the prejudices of the regulars. His Vicar-General and secretary, Fr. Barron, hearing that he told the facts to the provincial, and finding himself very much blamed in this city, had a mind to exculpate himself. On a meeting the clergy had about some affairs of marriage, confessed that he wrote that letter on said subject and other matters as he could not now avoid it being under obedience to the bishop. On which he and one Casey an Augustinian had some words of no great consequence. In short he suspended Casey and even assured him he would declare irregular if he said one Mass (the following day being Sunday) in the Augustinian chapel, unless he read publicly the following day from the altar such a recantation as was wrote by Barron, which Casey complied with. The bishop being then in the country, and hearing the town to be all inflamed, came to town and sent for the regular superiors, blamed them for maliciously inflaming the town, etc. I told his Lordship it was proceedings of his Vicar-General, his censures, and the recantation he ordered, made them come at the original cause and inflamed the town.

His Lordship began to exculpate himself by saying that he did not write to get the regulars secularised or suppressed which was maliciously said of him. I made him excuse that we never heard that he did about such terms, but that he wrote to get us removed from officiating in our own chapels and of consequence our residence could not subsist. His Lordship said that he only wished in his letter to the Pope that we were removed from our chapels and that it was rather a veleity than a wish or desire. He yesterday sent us a piece of writing to be read at all Masses, exculpating himself that he wrote nothing to Rome that could prejudice the regulars: but the regulars did not think proper to get the paper read as it was contrary to Fr. Barron's declaration and even to his own words. The provincial who parted Cork this day for Bordeaux in his way to Rome will tell you more. About 100 of the principal Roman Catholics of this city petition his Holiness on this subject in favour of the regulars: they address it to you. The regulars request that you will give a helping hand jointly with the provincial and other friends, and any expense you will be at

we will be willing to pay. Your care and activity in the above affair is expected by,

> Very Reverend Father Master,
> Your own assured humble servant,
> Dominic Morragh."

The petition, with its many signatures, dated 24 March 1774, and another from
the regular superiors of Cork, are preserved in the San Clemente archives in
Rome.

Within a decade Bishop Butler was involved in another dispute with the
regulars, and again a large number of prominent Cork citizens supported the
friars. The prior of the Augustinians at this time was Fr Liam Inglis, well known
as a poet in the Irish language. One of his poems had been inspired by his
expulsion from the Dominican Order in Cork, after he refused to comply with
the Preacher's rule of poverty. The Augustinians sympathised with him, and
accepted him as a novice. He went to Rome, and following ordination there in
1749, returned to Cork where he remained until his death in 1778.[71] He had
begun the building of a church in Brunswick Street, and the new prior, Fr
Edmond Keating, continued with this plan.

Bishop Butler objected to the building, as the new site was in a different
parish to that in which the friars had traditionally ministered. But Fr Keating, in
1780, proceeded with the plans, to the chagrin of the bishop.

The Ordinary addressed a strong message to the convened chapter of the
Order in June 1782, in which he emphasised that:

> "it was always our intention and (which dare venture to say will be con-
> firmed by the most sound and best members of the Order living in the City of
> Cork since our arrival therein) that we looked on the Order of St. Augustine
> as particularly under our protection, and that we always endeavoured to pro-
> mote the real interests of the Order, until we found that our good intentions
> were frustrated by the intrigues of the Revd. Mr. Keating heretofore prior to
> the Convent of Cork".

He warned the "Revd. and learned Chapter" that if they chose that "we should
continue our love and esteem for them . . . and if they think we should be
indulgent to them . . . they will exclude the said Revd. Mr. Keating from any
place of prominence among them, or in the city", and that they should elect
another prior.[72]

Dr Butler wrote in even more definite terms directly to Fr Keating a couple of months later. He ordered the friar "to quit this diocese under pain of

---

[70] *Coll. Hib.*, 1965, No.8, 107-9, quoting SCAR, Codex iv, doc.136.
[71] Ó Fiaich, Tomás, *Leachtaí Cholm Cille*, 1975, iv, 39.
[72] Battersby, W.J., *History of the Augustinians in Ireland*, 1856, 189-90.

suspension, as we hereby do declare him deprived of every jurisdiction". It was made clear that the prior had no further authority in the cloister, and that the bishop and senior friars who he named did not wish Fr Keating to remain a member of the convent.[73] However, the church building continued, and the bishop retaliated by suspending Prior Keating and his community. Now deprived of income, the Augustinians opened a school to provide for their sustenance. Again, as in the bishop's dispute with the Dominicans, there was considerable public support for the regulars. The principal Roman Catholics of the city certified that Fr Keating "for above ten years successively was resident in Cork; that we could never see or hear of anything reprehensible in his conduct, but he is a sober, prudent, exemplary clergyman". The other regulars in Cork also supported Fr Keating, and it is apparent from the considerable correspondence on the dispute that the bishop was mainly concerned with his authority over the regulars.[74]

The row was not resolved until Fr Keating journeyed to Rome and laid his case before the Pope. He secured papal approval for his work, and the Holy Father recommended that the Bishop of Cork should forgive his friars and proceed to bless the church.[75] The prior was restored to his community, and they resumed normal duties in the city.

Provincials of the regulars were at this time deeply concerned that their orders might become extinct; without novices, and subject to the authority of the bishops their morale was low.[76] In March 1783 Fr William Gahan, Provincial of the Augustinians, was endeavouring to remove three of his friars from Cork, but the bishop obstructed him. Dr Butler was within his rights, as Propaganda had ruled that regulars might only be moved with the Ordinary's consent. However, Fr Gahan felt that the bishop used this decree "to subvert religious discipline, to strike fear into the provincials of the religious orders, and exercise despotic power over the friars within his diocese . . .".[77] Propaganda refused to remove the decree, but urged the bishop to treat the friars "with love and justice"; the provincial was recommended to respect the bishop "as holy and undefiled".[78] Whether it was because of the Vatican's prompting or not, the bishop and the friar remained on good terms, and Fr Gahan was to remark in later times "I visited Lord Dunboyne in 1783, at his country seat in Monkstown, where he was pleased to favour me with his friendship, and seemed pleased to place some confidence in me".[79]

---

[73] A.P.F., S.C., *Irlanda*, vol. 15, f. 311–4, 319.

[74] A.P.F., S.C., *Irlanda*, vol. 15, f. 309, 315, 317–19, 321, 323. vol. 16, f. 92.

[75] Battersby, W.J., *History of the Augustinians in Ireland*, 1856, 189–90.

[76] Fenning, *Undoing*, 333 *et seq.*

[77] Ibid., 342–3.

[78] Ibid., 343.

[79] Gahan, *Testimony*, 8.

Whiteboyism regularly disturbed the county, and in July 1767 "Com. Lonergan was lodged in the county jail, charged with officiating as a popish priest, and with being concerned in a most insolent and seditious correspondence, relating to the Whiteboys in 1762, and containing his contempt of the laws and those appointed to execute them", according to a report in the *Freeman's Journal* of 28 July.

In 1776 a number of Whiteboys broke into the house of Dr Geoghegan, titular Bishop of Madaura and coadjutor of Meath. The *Hibernian Journal* of 1 April suggested that their intention was to rob and murder the bishop. But Dr Geoghegan was prepared and fired at the intruders, killing one of them and causing the rest to flee. It would seem that the bishop had drawn the odium of the Whiteboys by condemning them from the altar.

Unfortunately there is no record of the Bishop of Cork's reaction to a scandalous incident in 1780 which involved a priest and Lord Doneraile. It is reasonable to assume that Dr Butler knew both His Lordship and Fr Neale, who was described in contemporary newspaper accounts as a parish priest.[80] Doneraile was angry with the aged priest, who had excommunicated one of his tenants for living in adultery; he asked Fr. Neale to remove the excommunication, but he refused. The lord went to the priest's house and horsewhipped the priest and his "ancient maid servant" when she intervened. The case was brought to court, and Doneraile was fined £1,000; a couple of days later the priest died, and it was rumoured that now his lordship might be tried for murder. This did not happen, though the victim's defence had been in the hands of John Philpott Curran who had generously taken up the case when all the other lawyers on the circuit had shunned the brief. Thomas Davis believed that the priest's victory over the lord was "a conquest from the powers of darkness – the first spoils of emancipation".[81]

Another problem which occupied bishop Butler at this time was that of authority over Spike Island, in Cork Harbour; was it located in his diocese or in that of the adjoining Cloyne and Ross? Dr Butler II of Cashel decided that it was in Cork, in an effort to resolve the dispute between Bishop Butler and Bishop McKenna.[82] Despite the archbishop's ruling, and the intervention of Rome, Dr. McKenna did not accept the loss of his island, and the matter was not finally settled, in favour of Cork, until 1790 when John Butler was no longer concerned with the case.

The thirty-six year old Archbishop of Cashel, Dr James Butler II, who had been educated at the Jesuit College of St Omer in the north of France was, in 1778, involved in a bit of nepotism. He tried to have a relative, Fr John Butler, a former Jesuit, appointed as Bishop of Limerick. The archbishop of Dublin

---

80 Brady, *18th c. Press,* 210.
81 Ibid.
82 CBACE, 143.

strongly opposed this preferment for another of the Butler family, though Fr John was a son of Lord Cahir.[83] The Archbishop of Cashel's family, the Butlers of Ballyragget, like some of the Protestant landlords, claimed the right of provision to certain parishes. Dr Butler II could claim amongst his kinsmen the Kavanaghs of Borris and the Earls of Fingall. But the Cashel prelate was also concerned with his flock, and was endeavouring to bring about a revival of religious ceremonial in the archdiocese. He introduced a Confraternity, encouraged frequent attendance at Holy Communion, and he organised Corpus Christi processions. Bigoted persons, in 1780, charged the archbishop with "ringing the clergy of the Established Church into contempt. In your diocese the Established Church appeared tolerated, while the Church of Rome assumed uncommon usurpations . . . to carry this superiority to its full extent, you availed yourself of all family influence".[84]

Though the Bishop of Cork does not appear to have used his family position to further church affairs, he was active in ecclesiastical matters. For example, in September 1781, as noted in the *Cork Evening Post* of 17 September, he caused this exhortation to be read in all the city's chapels:

> "The Roman Catholics of this city are earnestly exhorted to maintain at all times, but particularly now when we are threatened by foreign enemies, a peaceable behaviour, and show their zeal and loyalty to his present majesty and government. They are to consider the military, that has been sent here for our defence, as their best friends and protectors; and so far from quarrelling with them, we strenuously exhort you to cherish and use them with every civility in your power, that by this and every demonstration, all our enemies may see that only one interest unites us, and that we are ready to sacrifice our lives and fortunes in support of this common cause."

He joined with the other Munster bishops on 16 July 1782 in sending a plea to the pope on behalf of the suspended Archbishop of Armagh, Dr Anthony Blake.[85] This prelate, from an old Galway tribe, appears to have been as attached to his family as was the Bishop of Cork. After his translation from Ardagh to Armagh he continued to reside among his relatives in the west, and only made statutory visits to his diocese. Some of his clergy complained to Rome, and he was suspended from his See. However, following an investigation by Dr Troy, then Bishop of Ossory, the primate was reinstated.[86]

In 1783 the question of Catholic loyalty to the throne was again being discussed, and the submission of addresses of loyalty to the king were consid-

---

[83] *Rep. Novum,* M.J. Curran, i, No. 2, 1956, 388.
[84] Renehan, *Collections,* 338-9.
[85] CBACE 147.
[86] CBACE, 196.

ered. Dr John Butler was rumoured to be in some way involved in the matter, but Archbishop Butler II assured the newly appointed Dr Troy of Dublin that the rumours about the Bishop of Cork were untrue. He believed that they were started by Fr O'Leary "who said that a Cork correspondent wrote to tell him that the Munster bishops were planning an address to His Majesty on the style of Sir Boyle Roche's".[87]

Dr Butler was interested in furthering the cause of the Catholic Committee, and in September 1782 the Treasurer of the Committee acknowledged the receipt of £160 from the Bishop of Cork and the Bishop of Cloyne and Ross. But, he added, much money will be required, even for day-to-day expenses.[88]

In 1784 John Butler was in Limerick on 1 May. There, as rumoured a year before, he joined with the other Munster bishops in a Declaration of Loyalty to the Government. They also exhorted their clergy to refrain from unlawful behaviour, as agitation could adversely effect further liberating legislation. The Munster bishops also sent a letter to Rome, protesting to the secretary at Propaganda Fide, that the Archbishop of Tuam was interfering in the administration of the diocese of Kilfenora, in the province of Cashel.[89]

Earlier the Bishop of Cork had assisted at the consecration of Dr Laurence Nihell, as Bishop of Kilfenora, in Limerick; the special preacher for the ceremony was Fr Walter Blake Kirwan, the greatest orator of the time.[90] That day he waxed eloquent on the subject of apostasy, an emotive subject in Ireland since at least 1567 when the Franciscan Miler Magrath, Bishop of Down and Connor, conformed to the Established church. His promotion, in due course, to the Sees of Clogher and Cashel, and his marriage to a Miss O'Meara, who bore him nine children, and remained a Catholic, did not lessen popular feelings towards him.[91] Fr Blake Kirwan's sermon did not refer to Archbishop Magrath, but as it was delivered in his celebrated style it had the desired effect of arousing the emotions of the congregation. One commentator felt that Fr Kirwan's sermons "were not remarkable for strength or pathos, but he was an incomparable actor".[92]

Another frequent subject for pulpit eloquence at this time was the condemnation of the widespread abuses practised at wakes. During the Synod of Cashel and Emly, held on 22 October, 1782 Archbishop Butler II of Cashel, presiding over the meeting of bishops at Thurles, issued the following Statute:

---

[87] PTAD, III, 140.
[88] CBACE, 148.
[89] CBACE, 155.
[90] Mitchell, James, *Galway Archaeological and Historical Society Journal,* 1974-5, XXXIV, 70.
[91] Wyse Jackson, R., *Archbishop Magrath,* 1974.
[92] Madden, D.O., *Revelations of Ireland,* 1877, 29.

"Since the original purpose of wakes was that the soul of the deceased might be helped by the prayers of those who attend, it is evident that this purpose is being defeated when immodest games are carried on, which suppress the memory of Death in the minds of those present. We . . . threaten with ex-communication everybody who takes part in this evil practice henceforth. Parish priests are to forbid their congregation to cover the mouth and nostrils of the dead person until they are certain that death has actually taken place, or to bury anybody until twenty-four hours after his death."[93]

Moral issues such as the wake abuses, drunkenness, agrarian violence, thieving and body-snatching would have demanded attention from the Bishop of Cork. Just before Christmas 1785, on a Sunday night, a group of Whiteboys, armed and aggressive, approached the parish priest of Ballyshoneen in county Cork and warned him, on pain of death, not to take more at any marriage than five shillings and five pence, and one shilling and seven pence at christenings. Some nights later the Whiteboys turned their attention to a parson, and cut the tails off his three fat cows and nailed them to the chapel door. The cows had to be killed.[94]

But Bishop John Butler also had his personal problems. His eldest brother, who had succeeded to the Dunboyne title in 1732, died unmarried in 1768. One of the brothers serving in France, Pierce, inherited, and came home. What, one wonders, were the feelings of Bishop John when Pierce became a Protestant in February 1769? Family troubles seemed to multiply: an unmarried sister died in 1778, and the only other woman of the family, Mrs Catherine O'Brien Butler, had been widowed in 1773. The new Lord Dunboyne initiated law proceedings to recover family property which had fallen into other hands, and these expensive and long drawn out litigations were to see him into the grave.

While he did regain ownership of Dunboyne Castle, at his death there in 1773 the lawyers were still engaged in further wrangling. Dr Butler lost his youngest brother in 1781, thus reducing the Dunboyne inheritance to the person of seven years old Pierce, only son of the late Lord Pierce.[95]

By this time the bishop fully realised the implications of these family bereavements, particularly as the child Pierce was not robust. He must have given considerable thought to the question of the Lordship of Dunboyne, and in Cork the gossips had already begun to speculate on what options were open to their Ordinary if his sickly nephew should die.

The story of a 16th century Butler lady must have been recalled and retold. She, when admonished by a clergyman on her deathbed as to certain duties which she should discharge before death, replied "It was better that one old

---

[93] Renehan, *Collections*, 479.
[94] Brady, *18th c. Press*, 231.
[95] *Com Peerage*, 1916, iv, 519.

woman should suffer the pains of another world, than that the Butlers should be left without an estate".[96] Perhaps even the bishop pondered on Lady Margaret's wisdom.

The Bishop of Cork's dilemma was intensified when the heir apparent also passed away. This is how Bishop John Butler's predicament was reported in the *Cork Hibernian Chronicle* of 22 December 1785: "a few days since, in Dublin, died Pierce Edmund Baron of Dunboyne, at.13; the title now devolves to his uncle, the Hon. and Rt. Rev. Dr. Butler R.C. Bishop of this Diocese". In January the *Hibernian Magazine* carried the notice: "Death. In the 13th year, Hon. Pierce Edmund, Lord Dunboyne; by his death title and estate to his uncle, John Butler, Catholic Bishop of Cork". He then also assumed the family arms, and the motto: *Timor Domini – Fons Vitae.*[97]

---

[96] Hall, Mr. & Mrs. S.C., *Ireland*, ii, 21.
[97] *Fear of the Lord – Source of Life.*

CHAPTER TWO

A Time of Decision

Once again agrarian outrages were disturbing Munster, and some of the agitators now insisted that tithes should be withheld from Catholic as well as Protestant clergymen. Dr Gerard Teahan, a future Bishop of Kerry, in a letter to the Archbishop of Cashel, dated 24 April 1786, wrote:

> "Lord Dunboyne, much to his honour, had early taken the alarm, on setting off to Dublin (to consult with the archbishop) he sketched out the letter and drew up the regulations of a pastoral letter immediately to be published in the different chapels of his diocese and in the public newspapers, had it appeared, it probably would have prevented all disturbances in this diocese and would further have had the good effect of being followed by similar regulations in the Diocese of Cloyne."[1]

Unfortunately, the Bishop of Cork's pastoral remained unpublished, due to the illness of the printer.[2] The position of the faith in the diocese of Cloyne, also in Co Cork, Teahan considered hopeless.

From Muskerry it was reported that some of the landlords had prosecuted the priests for extorting money from the people. In an effort to force their flocks to render their dues certain priests had refused to say mass, or to administer the sacraments, and as a result many people left the church altogether. Dr Teahan implored the archbishop to intervene, "to save the religion in Co. Cork",[3] that is in the area outside Dr Butler's diocese. Further pressure was placed on the archbishop on the following day, when a committee of Cork laymen, which had already consulted with both the Bishops of Cork and of Cloyne, asked him to come and sort matters out.[4]

Commenting on the situation on 27 March, the Cork Correspondent for the *Dublin Evening Post* of 6 April wrote:

> "the titular Bishops of Cork and Cloyne are, it is said, determined to institute

---

[1] CBACE, 158. Brady and Corish, *The Church under the Penal Code in A History of Irish Catholicism*. 1971, 55.

[2] Renehan, *Collections*. 346.

[3] CBACE, 158.

[4] Ibid., 159.

a most impartial and strict inquiry into the conduct of each parish priest in the respective dioceses; in such parishes where the people have declared their discontents, in order to redress them, and in the parishes where they have not yet murmured openly, to prevent their doing so hereafter."

Action was taken by the Munster bishops on 26 June, in Cork, when they drew up resolutions in an attempt to restore peace: two priests "who had become obnoxious to their people" were asked to resign, the extortion of dues was forbidden, as was the use of abusive language from the pulpit. Strong disapproval was voiced of parish priests who put their parishioners to excessive expense "by the entertainments provided at stations, weddings, christenings and funerals". Among the seven signatures to the paper is that of *Dunboyne.*[5] Butler was now correct in the use of the title, and henceforth he could be referred to as Baron or Lord Dunboyne. Indeed, as early as 19 January the Cashel prelate, in a letter to the Ordinary of Meath had written "I shall mention to Lord Dunboyne, whom I expect every day here, the character your lordship gives Rev. Mr. Smyth, which must entitle him to every mark of the good Bishop of Cork's attention".[6]

Another year was to elapse before the legal implications of the affairs of Dunboyne's late brothers were finalised, and he was in full control of the ancestral properties. It must have been a difficult time for the bishop with unrest in the diocese, and the additional worries of bereavement and future plans. According to the *Freeman's Journal* of 30 May 1786 "the Right Honourable Lord Dunboyne, who is also titular Bishop of Cork, took the Oaths of Allegiance in his Majesty's court of king's bench, as prescribed", which would indicate that he was already conforming to his new obligations.

In Cork, and further afield, rumours were rife about the Lord Bishop;[7] comparisons might have been made with the career and activities of the other mitred nobleman, Frederick Hervey, Earl of Bristol, and Protestant Bishop of Derry. Though an Englishman, Hervey had espoused many Irish causes since his appointment to the See of Derry in 1768. Anxious to improve the lot of Irish Catholics, he made frequent visits to the Vatican while travelling abroad, and on one occasion he was mistaken for a Roman Catholic prelate by the monks of the Great St Bernard. Though he lived mainly abroad, he supported the Volunteers when at home, and he gave considerable employment by embarking on the building of enormous mansions at Downhill and Ballyscullion. He was in Derry in the year that the Bishop of Cork inherited, but alas, there is no indication that the Lords Bishops exchanged views. Hervey, too, had family problems; his nephew, George Robert ("Fighting FitzGerald") FitzGerald, from

---

[5] CBACE, 159-160. Brady, *18th c. Press.* 234 *et seq.*
[6] Cogan, *Meath,* iii,III, 113.
[7] England, *Life,* 224.

Mayo, though a gentleman, had been hanged for murder. Lady Bristol and the bishop parted permanently in 1782, and he was said to have current ardent attachments to various other ladies.[8]

Bishop Butler's character was now similarly subjected to scrutiny; he was credited with several immoral liaisons in the past, and his life was rumoured to be "not very edifying". He was believed to see himself as "the last barren link of a long and distinguished race",[9] which, if so, would indicate on his part a serious lack of awareness of Dunboyne genealogy.

The Bishop of Cork was now faced with a grave personal decision: as a Catholic priest he was forbidden to marry, yet, if he did not, he believed that the future of the direct line in the lordship of Dunboyne was in danger of extinction (an interval of 140 years in the genealogical tree separated him from the next heir).[10] Like most old landed families, the Butlers were naturally anxious to see the continuance of the name and family fortunes, and the obvious way for Lord Dunboyne to ensure that he did not fail his obligations in this respect was to contemplate seeking a dispensation from Rome to enable him to marry. At this date the bishop was aged fifty-six, when he could still consider himself of marriageable age. His age was an important factor in later considerations of his conduct, as some writers have claimed that he was 67 or even over seventy years old when he inherited the title,[11] an age at which he might not have been so optimistic of fathering an heir. Various interpretations have been put on the Cork bishop's final decision to seek release from his vows from the Vatican. One Butler family historian argued that the bishop's intention was to prevent the lordship from coming into the Protestant end of the family, which he could have done if he produced an heir, and reared it as a Catholic himself.[12] Another authority claims that the aged prelate simply fell a victim to the wiles of a young Protestant cousin who, possibly with an eye to the title, set successfully about infatuating the holy man.[13]

In the parish of Drom, Co. Tipperary, a tranditional belief was that at Brookley House, a Butler residence, the bishop, while under the influence of drink, met Miss Maria Butler from Wilford, who encouraged his attentions. His lordship's coachman, who was present, discouraged Dunboyne's drinking

---

8   Fothergill, Brian, *The Mitred Earl*, 1974.

9   England, *Life*, 222-3.

10 Madden, D.O., *Revelations of Ireland*, 1877, 34.

11 Farrar, Henry, *Irish Marriages*, i, 1897, 136; Brady, W.M., *The Episcopal Succession in England, Scotland & Ireland: 1400-1875*, ii, 95; *Notes and Queries* (5th Series, Vol. 11th, January-June 1879), 1879, 31.

12 *Butler Jn.*, Hubert Butler, V, 1973-4, 378.

13 *Rep. Novum,* Sir Henry Blackhall, iii, No. 2, 1963-4, 371.

14 Butler, George, letter from the late. 23.3.1970. The only known portrait of the bishop was at Castle Crine, Co. Clare. The present Lord Dunboyne believes that it was destroyed about thirty years ago (see *Preface*.)

and encouraged him to leave, to no avail.[14] Whatever the motive behind his decision, Bishop Butler on 12 December 1786 resigned his See into the hands of the Pope, with this letter [15] in Latin:

> "Most Holy Father,
>
> Most humbly prostrate at the feet of your Holiness I pray and beg that you would deign to accept my pure and simple resignation of both the Diocese and the parish of St. Mary of this City of Cork. In making this petition I am moved by a two-fold motive. Firstly, because greatly reduced in strength I feel myself, in these most calamitous times, unequal to bearing such a load which already for more than twenty-three years up to now, I have endeavoured to bear. Secondly, because by succeeding to the inheritance and title of my family, I am so preoccupied by temporal cares that, as it were in a dilemma, I must necessarily neglect either Episcopal cares or temporal affairs. For which reason I again humbly beg Your Holiness that you would deign to accede to these requests of mine. Meanwhile I pray earnestly to the Great and Good God that He would deign to keep Your Holiness in good health for a long time.
>
> Most Holy Father,
Most devoted servant of Your Holiness
Dunboyne, Bishop of Cork
Cork 12 December 1786.

The lady whom the baron wished to make his baroness, and mother of his heir, was Maria Butler. She was twenty-three, and the younger daughter of a gentleman who resided at Wilford, Co. Tipperary.[16] She had conformed to the Established Church in 1773.[17]

Dunboyne had endeavoured to conduct his personal affairs as privately as possible, however, the faithful of the diocese were speculating as to his intentions. When he failed to attend a Profession at the Ursuline Convent in the city on 23 January 1787 his desertion of the See was confirmed, and the convent annalist, writing in a style typical of that time, made this entry in the records:

> 'The morning of this ceremony the fatal secret of Dr. Butler's prevarication began to transpire here. His Lordship, having had due notice of Sr. M. Ambrose Curtin's approaching Profession, promised as usual, to officiate at the ceremony. However when he understood that the most Holy Sacrifice of the Mass was to be offered in professing a novice a lingering sentiment of the fear of God deterred him from committing a new sacrilege. His apology arrived just as he was himself expected – the Novice was hurried off to write her vows

---

[15] A.P.F., S.C., Irlanda, vol. 16, f. 183.
[16] *Com.Peerage,* 1916, iv, 519.
[17] *Calendar of Convert Rolls,* i. 1703-1789, PRO.

Bishop Butler's letter to the pope, dated 12 December 1786

again, as they were drawn up first according to the form appointed for those who pronounce them in the presence of the Bishop.

The Rev. E. Synan, the Vicar General, performed the ceremony Sr. M. Ambrose received the black veil from his hands and those of the Mother M. Ursula Kavanagh, Superioress.

A short time after this, the long impending storm burst in the fall, the public fall of the unhappy Dr. Butler, who resumed his titles to the honours of the earth, and at the same time, resigned his claim to a place in heaven. This truly calamitous event spread consternation throughout the Monastery; the Superioress, Mother Mary Ursula Kavanagh a near relative of Lord Dunboyne, and the few beside who anticipated this catastrophe, were fatally convinced of the justice of their presentiments and overwhelmed with sorrow. As to the generality their astonishment was beyond conception; upon which it may be observed, that any sudden shock experienced here on the dire fall of Lord Dunboyne, is a strong proof, that before this period all must have been accustomed to consider in him not the man but the Bishop and Superior. Had this been otherwise the Religious should certainly have anticipated nearly as much as occurred, for the salt of the earth, had long before that lost its flavour. The conduct of Lord Dunboyne was in many instances such as should have made impressions to his disadvantage, in minds prepared to receive those impressions. No such minds were found here. To the last moment of Doctor Butler's appearance in this Monastery as a Bishop and Superior he was as reverenced as such and considered only with the eyes of faith-single obedience and Christian charity.[18]

Nevertheless, at the end of March, to judge from his correspondence, the Archbishop of Cashel was still ignorant of Dunboyne's intentions. Writing to his great friend Dr Plunkett of Meath he said "your lordship, no doubt, heard the reports circulated about Lord Dunboyne's resigning his bishopric. I am happy to assure you that they are all groundless".[19]

By the end of April, Baron Dunboyne had married Maria Butler, possibly in St. Mary's Church, Clonmel, though there is now no record of the ceremony there.[20] The Metropolitan of Cashel reported the outrage to Rome in a letter to Propaganda, dated 30th of that month, and delivered by his Vatican agent, Abbé James Connell:

> "It is not without the greatest sorrow that I tell how great a wound has been inflicted on the church through the unmentionable crime of John Butler, Baron of Dunboyne and Bishop of Cork, one of my subordinates. That unhappy man, with a degree of daring no less impious than sacrilegious, married a certain girl and with great scandal to the faithful lived publicly with her. I used every persuasion that zeal and prudence could offer to prevent such an outrage and bring the unfortunate man to repentance, but I laboured in vain, for his heart seemed immovable, and although he recognised the evil of his wedlock, still he persevered in it, deluded by the false hope that the pope would grant a dispensation to him to validate his marriage."[21]

---

[18] AUCC, i.

[19] Cogan, *Meath*, iii, 121.

[20] *Rep. Novum* John Kingston, iii, No. 1, 1961-2, 70.

[21] Ibid., 69-70.

Rome would seem to have been already familiar with the case as within a week, on 5 May, Cardinal Antonelli wrote to Cashel asking for a full report on the causes of the resignation, as the latter could not be accepted without the Vatican having the fullest details. A further problem for the Pope was the replacement of the Ordinary of Cork, and he gave thought to a petition from the regular clergy of that diocese that Bishop Moylan of Kerry should be translated to the vacant See.[22] There was a strong recommendation from the Archbishop of Dublin, the Archbishop of Tuam and the Bishops of Achonry and Clonfert that the Bishop of Kilfenora & Kilmacduagh, Laurence Nihell, should be sent to Cork. Dr. Nihell himself also applied for the transfer as "his present situation was proving harmful to his health, and that in Cork he would be in the vicinity of libraries and book shops and so would have a better opportunity of effectively pursuing his literary interests by the publication of apologetic works".[23] The Vatican, however, decided in favour of Bishop Moylan, while Dr. Teahan, who had so recently praised Dunboyne's firm action against the Whiteboys, became Bishop of Kerry. Cardinal Antonelli, in communicating these appointments to Cashel on 6 June, expressed the horror of the Roman authorities at Dr. Butler's apostasy. He exhorted the archbishop to use every possible means to bring the apostate to the right path, and to ensure that the church in Cork should suffer no evil as a result of the affair.[24]

The Archbishop of Cashel was also explaining matters to the Bishop of Meath in whose diocese Dunboyne may now have been resident. He had requested an immediate answer to his epistle seeking news:

> "I most gratefully acknowledge your letter, however melancholy the account be it conveys to me of my unhappy suffragan, I sit down, after quitting my clergy who were with me this day at a conference, to let you know that I highly applaud your conduct towards Lord Dunboyne, and quite agree with you that violent means are not immediately to be adopted. We must not extinguish the smoking flax, nor break the bending reed, everything must first be tried, but if the wound is incurable it must be cut off with the sword."[25]

The hieratic exchange of views, continued, with Dr. Caulfield, Bishop of Ferns, confiding to Dr. Troy on 9 May: I can't help feeling sorely with your Grace the severe stab given to the character of Irish clergy by the prevarication or corruption of a weak and withered limb of that body. We must put him down as St. John did the noted apostate of his day, "he went out from us, but was not of us". I suppose Dr. James of Cashel will issue an excommunication against him as his Metropolitan for a crime committed in his Province; and think it need not go

---

[22] CBACE, 164-5. Walsh, *Nagle,* 132.
[23] *Galway Arch. Soc. Jn.,* James Mitchell, XXXIV, 1974-5, 76.
[24] CBACE, 164-5.
[25] Cogan, *Meath,* iii, 123.

farther but let the Prelates in whose diocese he shall be notify it to their clergy for their Government towards him, if he shall attempt any communication with any of them. I believe the less noise is made otherwise about him, the better. I know the sound of his now inglorious name hurts me.[26]

There is a tradition in the Stradbally area of Co. Leix that the Dunboynes spent their honeymoon at Ballythomas House, between that town and The Heath. A tree-lined path there is still remembered as "the bishop's walk", in memory of his visit. This version of the story has been recorded: "It is stated that Lord Dunboyne, Bishop of Cork, lived here in seclusion, subsequent to his apostasy. The old natives tell of his woe-begone appearance, and of his stealthy walks down by the hedge-rows, to recite the Divine office". Ballythomas, a 17th century mansion, was at the time owned by a Fitzgerald family. It is still recalled in the locality that during the Dunboynes' first night in the house either a dead cat or a dog was hung from the doorknob.[27]

The national sensation caused by the marriage of a Roman Catholic clergyman soon began to reflect itself in the press, both in Cork and Dublin. At this period the country was blessed with an abundance of newspapers. They carried news from London and abroad, official announcements, and advertising. Home affairs were also covered, and much space might be devoted to religious and philosophical discussions. Events of a sensational or of a scandalous nature were reported, very often in the form of innuendoes. It was quite usual to reprint material from other papers, with an acknowledgement. On 10 May 1787 the *Cork Hibernian Chronicle* reported an innovation in the treatment of minor offenders in the city; one Catherine Hodnett, convicted of petty larceny, was publicly exhibited in several parts of the town, "on our new moving pillory". A description of this useful apparatus followed. Competing with the mobile pillory for attention was this veiled reference to the Dunboyne affair; quoted in the Cork paper, from the *Dublin Evening Herald*:

> "The report that a certain Roman Catholic nobleman, who is also a Titular Bishop, has conformed to the established religion still gains ground and has caused various speculations in this city, if his lordship acted from motives of religion, and he believed the principals he professed were contrary to the dictates of his conscience we cannot sufficiently applaud his motives; but if on the contrary he thirsted after the pomps and vanities of this wicked world, and that his heart gave the lie to the words he expressed with his lips, we can only lament the depravity of human nature, that hurries even our greatest men to commit actions which the poorest peasant, in his humble hut, would

---

[26] PTAD, I, 24, I.

[27] Comerford, M. *Collections relating to the Dioceses of Kildare and Leighlin*, III, 282. For further details of local traditions I am indebted to the late Rev. P. Harris, PP, Naas, Rev. G. Brophy. PP, Portlaoise, Mr. E. Boylan, Miss B. Dooley, Mr. J. Phelan, Portlaoise.

shudder to mention; and convinces us that while we suffer our passion to triumph over our reason and understanding, we are no better than the most abandoned libertines, whose work is destruction and whose God is their belly."

On the same date the *Dublin Chronicle* commented:

'It is the prevailing report of the day, that the marriage of a Roman Catholic nobleman, who is also a titular bishop, has happened in consequence of a dispensation from the Pope, as with the death of this nobleman the title would become extinct, and the fortune devolve to the crown. Many modern instances of a similar nature might be adduced, and therefore this conjecture or as it is said authentic information, must gain some degree of general credit, as there has been no recantation of religion in the case, a very few days will however clear up this whole affair, and reduce the fact to an absolute state of certainty."

Two days later the paper was more explicit:

"The marriage of Lord Dunboyne is one of the most singular events which has happened for many centuries. So complete a dereliction of Papal Authority in a personage so exalted in title and ecclesiastical dignity, has diffused a gloom of discontent through the Roman Catholics; the example it is supposed will be productive of an almost general imitation, especially among such ecclesiastics as are either already possessed of a competency, or expected by marriage to obtain one. The cases of Henry the 8th of England and the present Lord Dunboyne are nearly similar. Henry solicited the court of Rome for a divorce from Queen Catherine and permission to marry Anne Bullen, and was refused. Lord Dunboyne applied to the same court for a divorce from Mother Church and dispensation to marry Miss Butler. His suit was also rejected. It is unnecessary to add, that regardless of Papal Anathemas, they both gratified their respective desires - the parallel extends even farther, for though Henry effectually scouted the Pope's authority out of England, still he continued a violent bigot, to the other tenets of the Roman Church, and we do not find that my .Lord Dunboyne has yet conformed, notwithstanding the contempt he has shown for the Sovereign Pontiff, by entering into the connubial state contrary to his express commands."[28]

The same journal also carried the rather cryptic information:

We hear that a noble lord lately married is writing a learned commentary on the words Salvo Meo Ordine,[29] in which he disproves the meaning affixed to them by Dr. Butler, Mr. O'Leary and other controversialists, who have lately

---

[28] Brady, *18th c. Press,* 253.
[29] *Safeguarding my own rank.*

expended so much criticism in their explanation; his lordship shows that Ordine literally signifies Family Title; and that a Popish bishop's consecration Oath ceases to be obligatory when it tends to shift the bishop's title or fortune to a collateral branch of his family.

The financial reward given to priests who went over to the Established Church, if they did not get an appointment, was a maintenance of £40 a year for which they were "expected publicly to read the liturgy of the Church of Ireland in English, in such places and at such times as the archbishop or bishop shall direct".[30]

While the prediction of mass apostasies did not prove accurate, it did coincide with a peak-period of clerical desertions. During the 18th century sixty priests apostatised, though Fr. Finegan, S.J. believed that the number may be larger. Before 1749 only three priests conformed, while between 1751 and 1799 the total was fifty-seven, possibly due, in the Jesuit's opinion "to indifferentism which they must have experienced during their sojourn on the continent".[31]

In Cork during the time that John Butler ministered there (1758-1787) newspaper reports show that two priests and 30 laymen or women renounced the Church of Rome. Sometimes the motives of the neophytes were given, such as to have the benefit of freeholders to vote at any ensuing election for members of parliament, and to be on grand juries. But one Bridget Welsh, from Lord Dunboyne's local town of Fethard, recanted in 1768 "in order to qualify her to be married to an eminent shoemaker of said place".[32]

However, within a month of the forecast by the *Dublin Chronicle* there was another remarkable defection from the Roman fold, in the church of St. Peter in Dublin, when Fr. Walter Blake Kirwan, who had spoken austerely on the horrors of apostasy in the presence of the former Bishop of Cork some four years previously, himself abandoned Rome for the Established Church.

This is how the *Faulkner's Dublin Journal* reported the matter on 23 June 1787:

> "On Sunday last, the Rev. Walter Blake Kirwan of the order of St. Francis, and nephew of the Rev. Doctor Blake, titular Archbishop of Armagh, conformed publicly to the Established Church in St. Peter's, Dublin. He was accompanied and conveyed to church by the Right Rev. the Lord bishop of Cloyne, and received the Sacrament from the hands of the Rev. Archdeacon of Dublin, who preached an excellent and truly Christian sermon upon the occasion.

Kirwan preached in St. Peter's Church on the following Sunday, and he con-

---

[30] 19 and 20 Geo. III, 1779-80.
[31] Finegan, Francis, S.J., *Studies*, XXXVIII, 1949, 81.
[32] Brady, *18th c. Press*, 131.

tinued as the regular Sunday preacher there for a year. He married, and ministered in the parishes of St. Nicholas-Without and of Howth, before he was
appointed Dean of Killala in 1800. Whether the example of Lord Dunboyne
had served as encouragement to Fr. Blake Kirwan must be surmised, but he
claimed, in a "letter to a friend in Galway", published in the *Dublin Evening Post*
on 19 June 1787, that his decision was to enable him to render "more service to
the community".[33]

Fr. Kirwan's apostasy was all the more sensational as he was a nephew of
the controversial Roman Catholic Primate of Armagh, Archbishop Blake, though
the then retired prelate commented on the perversion: "Tut, tut, the man never
had a religion to lose".[34] A younger brother of Kirwan's was also a priest, in
Galway, and a false rumour claimed that he had "died of grief, occasioned by
the circumstances", though, in fact, he lived for another fourteen years.[35]

By coincidence, on the day following Kirwan's public apostasy, the behaviour of the former Bishop of Cork was subject to censure in his own city. At a
meeting of the Ven. John's Society,[36] held on 25 June, this minute was recorded:

> "It was resolved unanimously by the Members then present – that whereas
> this respectable Society has had the afflicting mortification of finding itself
> dishonoured by the Impiety and Sacrilege which one of its members, Lord
> Dunboyne, has been guilty of, in order to express our just abhorrence of his
> conduct, it is resolved that he be expelled, and he is hereby expelled from this
> Society."[37]

The minute books of this society of laymen, of which the Catholic Bishop of
Cork was then chairman by rotation, date back to 1783; it still flourishes.

In the 18th century the ballad maker was at hand to set every notable event
to verse, and soon broadsheets entitled *A Ballad of John, Lord Dunboyne, Bishop
of Cork"*[38] were on sale in the streets. This is the message they carried:

> Let the Catholic Church be now arrayed
> In deep disconsolation!
> Let her banners sad be now displayed
> Throughout each Christian Nation!
> At the Isle of Saints a bishop there

---

[33] Kirwan, W., *A discourse on religious Innovations*, 1787.

[34] Finegan, Francis S.J., *Studies*, XXXVIII, 1949, 81.

[35] *Galway Arch. Soc. Jn.,* James Mitchell, XXXVIII, 1974-5, 71.

[36] This Society was founded to counteract Jansenism, and at the meetings the Members declared when they had last received the sacraments.

[37] Minutes of the Ven. John's Society, Cork, 1787.

[38] *Butler Jn.*, ii, 1969, 91-2.

Has lost his consecration
And a pillar great has fell of late
By Satan's operation
In Cork of late for a small estate
A spiritual lord revolted
From that noble ecclesiastical state
To which the Pope exalted.
Not born a member of the Church of Rome,[39]
To Luther he did adhere,
From darkness to our Church he came
And to darkness did retire.
From our bright faith you did retreat
And joined the court of Venus.
Profligate, void of every hope,
You threw off the robe of Jesus.
Your power was greater than St. John's
Who did baptise our Saviour:
For you could take Him in your hands,
Then why did you forsake Him?
I'm sure you're worse than Henry the Eighth
Who put away his consort
Your virtuous spouse you did forsake
When the Holy Church you abandoned.
As the shepherd now is gone astray
God keep the flock from random
That on the great accounting day
His blood may prove our ransom.
Now sure you know there is one God
By whom we are all created.
And sure you know there is but one Faith
By which we are consecrated;
And sure you know there is but one Ark
To keep us from desolation;
And sure you know there is but one Church
Can ever expect salvation.

Another, longer version of this ballad, called *Bishop Butler's Reformation* was also circulated; it differed from the other in one important point, as it claimed that the bishop was "born a member of the Church of Rome".[40] Early in the 19th century Michael Carolan translated into Irish a version of these two ballads, under the title *Bishop of Cork falls from the Catholic Church*.[41] In Clonmel there

---

[39] There is no evidence for this claim
[40] *Broadside Ballads.* L.O. National Library.
[41] RIA, MS 24, P. 7, 262-5.

BISHOP
BUTLER'S
REFORMATION.

LET the Catholic Church be now arrange'd in deep
   disconsolation,
Let her mourning banners be now display'd throughout each christian nation,
In the Isle of Saints, a Bishop there, has lost his consecration,
A piller great, that fell of late, by Satan's operation.

In Cork of late, for a small estate, a spiritual lord re-
      volted,   (Pope exalted;
From the Ecclesiastical noble state, to which the
Born a member of the Church of Rome, with Luther
   he did hire,   (did retire.
From darkness to our church did come & to darkness

Lust and mammon did him seduce, when he left our
   holy alter,
The sacrement you did abuse, by quitting holy orders
Your power was greater than St. John's, when he bap-
     tized our Saviour,   (you forsake him.
You elevated him between your hands, and why did

You should mortify the flesh, when you found these
   passions rising,
Constantly to fast and pray when Satan you are facing
You should invoke the holy saints, to pray for your
   salvation,   (exempt you from d—,
That your prayers might quell, the flames of h—, &

Our Church was built against a rock, and founded by
   our Saviour,   (against her,
The gates of h—, in regions dark, shall not prevail
She is a ship, that can't be wreck'd, or ever drown a
   sailor,   d— for ever.
But each as plunges from her deck, their sunk and

I'm sure you know by one God we are all created
I'm sure you know by one faith we're all consecrated
I'm sure you know by one ark we escaped from dis-
   solution   (salvation
And Christ promised but one church wherein to find

It was through despair that Judas fell when he betra-
   yed our Saviour   (life for ever
The repenting thief that God absolved and gave h.
If you repent grieve and lament, & make your refor-
   mation   salvation
Mercy for justice shall contend and plead for your,

The opening verses of the ballad sheet Bishop Butler's Reformation

was a lampoon on Dunboyne, part of which went *In St. Mary's church, Clonmel,*
by candle, by book and by knell.[42] The subject of apostate priests provided rich
material for both poets and satirists in the native language. The mother of one
such cleric Dominic Ó Domhnaill from Raphoe, is said to have composed a
lament, of which this is part:

> Nuair a bhéas tu i nIfrionn go fóill,
> Agus na deora ag sileadh leat.
> Sin an áit a bhfuigh tú na sgéala,
> Cia'ca's fearr sagart nó ministear.[43]

> (When you are yet in Hell
> shedding tears,
> that is where you will discover
> which is better, priest or minister.)

---

[42] Tradition from Mr.K. Fennessey, Curator, Clonmel Museum, 12.12.1975.
[43] Wall, Maureen, *The Penal Laws, 1691-1760*, 1967, 38.

CHAPTER THREE

Papal Reaction

I n the meantime news from the Vatican reached Ireland. During the month of June it was learned reliably, from Fr Valentine Bodkin, that all in Rome were grieved, and that when His Holiness, Pope Pius VI, read the Bishop of Cork's letter of resignation and petition to marry, "he wept openly".[1] Having considered the problem, on 9 June the Pope had composed a long and forceful reply to Dunboyne, and it was enclosed in Bodkin's package to the archbishop of Cashel. The Holy Father, in a letter to Cashel, deplored the apostasy and the public scandal which it caused. The archbishop, implored the Pope, "must use every means to convert the apostate from his sinful life of concubinage".[2] The Archbishop of Dublin was being kept informed independently of the happenings by his agent in Rome. Writing on 13 June Fr Charles O'Kelly O.P. told Dr Troy that:

> "The unhappy Dunboyne wrote to me, to apply to the Pope for a dispensation to marry. He did not wait for my answer, which I addressed to you for greater security of his receiving it. Therein I said all that occurred to me to divert him from his sacrilegious and scandalous purpose. Cashel informed the Pope officiously of his fall. Propaganda by order of his holiness wrote a paternal letter either to himself immediately or to Cashel, to reclaim him. I cautioned Borgia not to give you any commission about him."[3]

About a month later the Bishop of Ferns wrote to Dr Troy to tell him of some of the reports circulating about Dunboyne, and to ask for news of the matter:

> "For God's sake, have you any news about unfortunate Dunboyne or the See of Cork? Here the reports are various but melancholy, one, that he went to Scotland to legalise his whoring, another that he is tired of his doxy and will quit. Another, that he weeps the whole morning and drowns sorrow in the evening in bumpers of claret. My apprehension for the wretched man is that he never had any truly Christian feeling, or if he had, that his scandalous prevarication has stifled it, and I fear, that in just chastisement, the divine

---

[1] CBACE, 166.
[2] Ibid., 165.
[3] PTAD, I, No. 15, 2-3.

judgement will leave him to his own reprobate sense. The world is scandalised that he is not censured, thinking that he is only screened by his fortune and rank, which make his foul crimes the more glaring".[4]

Further pressure from Rome was being applied to the Metropolitan of Cashel. Writing on 16 June Cardinal Antonelli advised the archbishop to work for the conversion of the apostate bishop, especially as the Pope was concerned over the scandal. Also, the authorities wanted to know what censures they should impose on the ex-bishop? A week later Cardinal Salviati informed Cashel that the scandal was a cause of great sorrow to everyone, and though a new bishop had been appointed, hope of converting Dr Butler must not be abandoned.[5]

Some time elapsed before the archbishop could arrange a meeting with the recalcitrant cleric. Eventually, Lord Dunboyne agreed to meet his former Metropolitan at the house of a mutual friend, Dr Fogarty of Clonmel, on 11 August, to receive the papal letter of 9 June.[6] At the appointed time the archbishop arrived at Dr Fogarty's to find Dunboyne was already there.

Lord Dunboyne opened the parchment, and read with attention:

"It is not to be believed, venerable brother, with what consternation and anguish of mind We have been seized and overwhelmed, ever since We have received authentic information, that such was the height of infatuation which your mis-conduct had reached, that you intended to espouse a Protestant female; and dare, even now, to live with her in a state of most disgraceful concubinage. It seemed unto us, like some portentous visitation from Heaven, that a person, who had for above three and twenty years filled the station of a bishop, should, at this moment so far disregard the holy laws - so far disregard the episcopal character and his own, so as to involve himself in such a depth of shame, to inflict on the Church so gross an outrage, and consciously and voluntarily, to plunge his own soul into utter perdition. Truly We shudder With horror at this flagitious proceeding; nor can We now, from - the intense agitation of our feelings, find words competent to express our indignation, at such an excess of depravity. Yet, amidst the variety of painful emotions which it has excited – of grief, amazement, detestation, anxiety, and affliction; far ascendant above the rest, and predominate in Our bosom, is a truly paternal commiseration for yourself, and an ardent longing to rescue you, if possible, from such an abyss of profligacy and wretchedness.

With this view, Our first impulse is, to implore for you the mercy of God, and earnestly to entreat, and through His Son, Our Lord Jesus Christ, to supplicate of Him, to recall you to your genuine feelings, to inspire you with contrition and penance for your transgression, and, in His pity, to grant you the desire of emerging from your debasement; a heartfelt sorrow, and an

---

4 PTAD, I, No. 27, 2-3.
5 CBACE, 166.
6 England, *Life,* 231.

Venerabili Fratri Joanni Episcopo Corcagiensi

Pius PP. VI

Ven: Frater Salutem. Incredibile est, Ven: Frater, qua ad
miratione correpti, quoque Animi
dolore oppressi simus, ex quo No
bis certo allatum est Nuncio, Te ad
eam vesaniam devenisse, ut Ma
trimonium inire cum quadam
etherodoxa Muliere volueris, cum
eaque nunc vivere in turpissi-
mo Concubinatu non verearis.
Id Nobis portenti simile visum
est, ut qui in Episcopatu plus
quam tres et viginti transegit
Annos, nunc Sacrarum Legum
sui Episcopalis Caracteris, denique
sui met ipsius ita oblitus sit, ut
tale in Se susceperit dedecus,
talemu in Ecclesiam offensionem
intulerit, ac Animam Suam in
tale, tantumque exitium sciens,
us =

Part of the letter from Pope Pius VI to the Bishop of Cork,
dated 9 June 1787

abundant flow of tears, wherewith to wash away your iniquities, and repair your scandals; and finally to withdraw you from paths of perdition, by a sincere conversion.

Wherefore, We summon, We address, and beseech you, brother, fairly to view your condition, to abhor and bewail your wickedness, lest in the end, you draw upon yourself the most dread of God's judgements, which yet remains suspended; and, meanwhile, expose yourself to the heaviest chastisement of your offence, namely to be abandoned by the divine grace in the midst of your delinquency, and when sunk deepest in guilt, to be least sensible of its enormity.

Recollect what you were discharging, the functions of a bishop, and what even now you are, clothed as you still continue to be with that dignity which you so much dishonour and pollute. With all the warmth of zeal, therefore, which Our pontifical character calls upon Us to exert, We exhort you and beseech you, brother in the Lord, to awaken and arise. We admonish, We reprove, and rebuke you, and bring to Our aid every office and ministry of paternal love, solicitude, and correction to rouse, to elevate, and inflame you – miserably prostrate as you are, to the thoughts of salvation and the necessity of repentance.

But if, which God forbid! you slight the stings of conscience; if you remain deaf to the invocation of this warning voice, and persist in the mire and turpitude of so opprobrious a life, it will be Our imperative duty, of which we give you this denunciation and solemn notice, to assume the part and enforce the measures prescribed by the sacred Canons, measures with which, after having so long exercised the offices of bishop, you cannot be unacquainted.

In conclusion, We reiterate Our supplication to God, to imbue you with the spirit of amendment and compunction; and in the auspicious confidence that His mercy will be extended to you, We most cordially, venerable brother bestow on you Our apostolic benediction."[7]

News of Dunboyne's response to the papal brief does not appear to have been widespread, as a week after the meeting between the two Butler prelates the Bishop Elect of Ossory was informing the Archbishop of Dublin that:

> 'The brief for the infamous Dunboyne is arrived, it is feeling, nervous and authoritative, but it concludes with a menace, which, I apprehend, will make him break off with the church. This instrument is as yet kept a profound secret. I presume his Grace means to hand it himself in person to the ignoble peer, who is at present in the vicinity of Thurles. God grant that the sight of this shameless concubinarian may not injure the health of the archbishop and renew his late complaints."[8]

Little did Dr Dunne know that on the day following the writing of this epistle

---

7 A.P.F., S.C., Irlanda, 16, f. 326 *et seq.*
8 PTAD, I. No. 30, 2–3.

the "ignoble peer, the infamous Dunboyne" was to make the final move in his scheme to ensure the future of his noble house.

Later the Archbishop of Cashel requested the bishop of Waterford and Lismore, William Egan, whom he considered a man of "enlightened mind", to endeavour to influence the apostate.[9] Bishop Egan had lived in Clonmel since 1751, and would have been familiar with Dunboyne and his predicament. However, there is no record of his efforts to reconcile the Baron, which obviously were unsuccessful.

With all this unpleasantness and scandal it is not surprising that the Archbishop of Cashel was ill by December of that year and, just before Christmas, Dr Caulfield in a letter to Dr Troy admitted that he was alarmed for Dr Butler, fearing that he had "harrassed his mental faculties too much".[10]

Archbishop Butler's troubles were not to cease with the passing of 1787. In the following year, when his brother died, he succeeded to the family estate of Ballyragget. Dr Butler arranged for the property to be managed by his younger brother George, while he himself continued to live in Thurles with an annual income of £1,000 from Ballyragget. With the money he built a new episcopal residence in Thurles, and a parochial house in Cashel.[11] In addition to these worthwhile memorials James Butler is remembered as the writer of a Catechism in 1777 which, in a revised edition by JKL (Bishop Doyle of Kildare and Leighlin), was reprinted as late as 1929, and remained the standard work for schools long after that date.[12]

His memorial in Thurles recalls that "the most illustrious and most reverend lord, Lord James Butler, sprung from the most noble family of Ormonde, who, disregarding this world's attractions, gave himself wholly to God. Consecrated unwillingly Archbishop of Cashel, he governed and instructed during seventeen years the province of Munster with piety, wisdom, and apostolical zeal, discharging his duty to God, his sovereign, and his country. Truly philanthropic and humble, he was as a pastor of prelates an honour and an example".

The Rev. Mr Donlevy, curate of St. Mary's Church, Clonmel, conducted the morning service on Sunday, 19 August 1787[13] during which Lord Dunboyne went through the procedures for recanting. During the taking of the Oaths Baron Dunboyne was visibly nervous and inaudible. When the curate motioned him to a side table, to sign the Roll of Allegiance and Supremacy, and

---

[9] England, *Life*, 232.

[10] PTAD, iv, No. 37.

[11] CBACE, 59. Bowden, Charles, *Tour through Ireland, 1791*, 198.

[12] Wallace, P., *Irish Catechesis* - the heritage from James Butler II, Archbishop of Cashel. A dissertation submitted to the Faculty of the School of Religious Studies of the Catholic University of America, for the Degree Doctor of Philosophy. Washington D.C. 1975.

[13] Gahan, *Testimony*, 5.

St. Mary's Church, Clonmel, where Bishop Butler recanted

the Roll containing the Declaration against Popery,[14] he leant on the table as if for support. The service continued, and the neophyte took Communion before he himself administered the sacrament to the congregation.

The procedure by which Lord Dunboyne conformed to the Established Church was laid down in an Act (21, 22 George 3) of 1781. This legislation updated the old procedures and rendered "the manner of conforming from the Popish to the Protestant religion more easy and expeditious". By it a convert from Popery was "to be deemed Protestant if he received the sacrament according to the established church on any Sunday in any parish, and took and subscribed the Oaths of Allegiance, Supremacy and Abjuration, and the declaration, before the same minister in any convenient place, and filed the certificate given by the minister in chancery within six months", for which the fee was six pence. The Oaths administered to Lord Dunboyne were substantially the same as those to which he had subscribed in 1778 and 1786. The Declaration which he completed would have been as follows:

"I, John Butler, do solemnly and sincerely in the presence of God profess,

---

[14] *Calendar of Convert Rolls,* i. 1703-1789, PRO.

testify, and declare: That I do believe, that in the sacrament of the Lord's-Supper there is not any transubstantiation of the elements of bread and wine in the body and blood of Christ at or after the consecration thereof by any person whatsoever; and that the invocation or adoration of the Virgin Mary, or any other saint, and the sacrifice of the mass, as they are now used in the church of Rome, are superstitious and idolatrous. And I solemnly in the presence of God profess, testify, and declare, that I do make this declaration, and every part thereof, in the plain and ordinary sense of the words read unto me, as they are commonly understood by Protestants, without any evasion, equivocation, or mental reservation whatsoever; and without any dispensation already granted me for this purpose by the Pope, or any other authority or person whatsoever, or without any hope of dispensation from any person or authority whatsoever, or without believing that I am, or can be, acquitted before God or man, or absolved of this declaration, or any part thereof, although the Pope or any other person or persons, or power whatsoever, shall dispense with or annul the same, or declare that it was null and void from the beginning."

Word had got abroad about the apostasy. Since Christmas, when the resignation of John Butler from the See of Cork had become common knowledge, the country was rife with rumours. Some stories claimed that long before he inherited the title he had been prone to immoral living, and to neglecting his flock.[15] He was said to be proud, drunken and violent of temper; the twenty-three years of his occupancy of the See were fine-combed for derogatory incidents.

No sooner had the Butlers entered St Mary's on 19 August than word had spread throughout Clonmel; some of the more curious townsfolk began to congregate near the church, while those more critical of the bishop's intentions came close to the door to try and follow the progress of the service. Even they were reluctant to enter the church and interrupt the religious happenings. Apart from a few whistles and cat-calls they remained quiet until the door of St. Mary's opened and Lord Earlsfort, followed by Lord and Lady Dunboyne, left the church.[16] Shouting abuse, the mob obstructed the carriage and hailed turf, potatoes and lumps of dung at the party as they quickly entered the carriage and were driven off at speed.[17]

This unpleasant occurrence may have reminded Lord Dunboyne of an incident in Longford some sixteen years before when, on Easter Sunday 1770, two men interrupted service in the parish church during which the local Catholic curate had recanted and was about to receive communion; or of the fate of Fr Barnabas O'Farrell after he recanted. On the 14 March 1779 Dr O'Farrell preached in Dublin's historic St Michan's church on his reasons for abjuring

---

[15] Healy, *Maynooth*, 297, England, *Life*, 224.
[16] PTAD, I, No. 18.
[17] Ibid.

the tenets of the Church of Rome. The church, churchyard and streets leading to the Liffey were packed with people, so much so that, according to the *Hibernian Journal* of 17 March, the church gallery was falling "which made several persons of both sexes throw themselves out of the windows, and it was at length thought necessary to procure a guard to surround the pulpit and defend the clergyman from the rudeness of some of the mob". Later the priest was assaulted as he went down the quays, forcing him to take refuge in a shop. Over a year later he was again attacked in the street, and though there were several witnesses, no one came to his aid.[18]

Another renegade priest also met violence on the Dublin city quays some five years after he had recanted in Monaghan. James M'Mahon was walking on the North Wall when some coal porters unloading a ship started to jeer him; he drew a short sword and stabbed a master porter, who died at once. M'Mahon was lodged in Newgate, and later found guilty of manslaughter.[19] Not until the parish priest of Kilmalkedar renounced Rome in Dingle church in 1844 did an apostasy cause such a sensation as that of the Bishop of Cork. It was rumoured that Lynch Law was going to be executed on Fr. Brasbie, but, as the *Kerry Evening Post* later reported:

> "the townspeople were astonished to see the Hon. Captain Plunkett, of H.M. steamer *Stromboli*, march into town from Ventry, with a force of about 100 men, including the Marine Artillery and Marines, with drums and colours. The fine body of men, armed to the teeth, having joined the seamen and Marines of H.M. brigantine the *Lynx*, under the command of Captain Nott, presented such an imposing appearance, that, we need scarcely say, everything passed off very quietly. The Coast Guards from the surrounding stations were marched to Church, fully armed, and conveyed the Rev. Gentleman to the house of the Rev. Mr. Gayer, where he at present remains. Mr. Gillman, our active sub-inspector, had all his police ready to turn out at a moment's notice. Dingle, for the last 20 years, never presented such a force".

The Rev. Brasbie also married, and he later caused the college at Maynooth considerable discomfort when he sued the President there for "a gross and malicious libel". Like Dr Butler, he was lampooned widely in Irish, but unlike his lordship, he did not live openly at home. As he did not enjoy the privileges of wealth and position like Lord Dunboyne he found it expedient to emigrate to Canada, where he died in obscurity.[20]

News of the former Bishop of Cork's apostasy was quickly relayed to the Metropolitan at Cashel, and he hastened to report to Archbishop Troy of Dub-

---

[18] Brady, *18th c. Press*, 139.

[19] Ibid., 169, 171.

[20] De Brun, Padraig, *Journal Kerry Archaeological and Historical Society,* ii, 1969, 38 *et seq.*

lin, enclosing a copy of the Pope's plea to Dunboyne. In a letter dated 22 August he wrote:

> 'I have the honour of transmitting to your Grace a copy of his Holiness's letter to Lord Dunboyne. Happy would I transmit at the same time an account of the desired impression it made on the unhappy man's heart; but alas! Pharaoh's heart is hardened. . . . Last Sunday, before the close of the assizes in open contradiction to all that ought to be expected from the Pope's most affecting letter to him, he went in the most public manner to Church in Clonmel and read his recantation. Your Lordship I am convinced sympathises with me in this melancholy event, an event which gave the very day the highest scandal in Clonmel. The populace were so shocked at it, that they gathered round his carriage and pelted him with all that came to their hands, so much had it not been for Lord Earlsfort's taking him into his coach I doubt what would have become of him. The abuse he met with from the rabble and the rough manner he was handled by the lawyers during the trial of a lawsuit between him and a Mr. Cooke of Kiltinan ought to have awakened him to a sense of what he had to fear from the vengeance of God, but it seems he is proof to all that can terrify. I can't but look on it as a particular disposition of providence towards us that at the same time as it visited us with so severe a trial, it was pleased to manifest to the whole country that the apostasy of the unhappy man originated from the corruption of his heart, and not from conviction of reason".[21]

The parish priest of Cashel, Very Rev. Thomas Bray, reported the defection to the Abbé Bodkin in Rome: ". . . I delayed only so as to be able to inform you of something decisive and positive about that truly disgraced and iniquitous 'My Lord Dunboyne, John Butler (former Bishop of Cork)'. And I so have to tell you that this last Sunday he capped the pinnacle of his iniquity with apostasy, and in the Church of Clonmel at a General Communion of Co. Waterford, he abjured the Catholic faith publicly and received the Sacrament according to the Rite of the Anglican Church of Protestants. You yourself can easily conclude what deep and intense sorrow we have suffered."[22]

Dr Troy was also informed of the outrage by other correspondents. The Bishop of Ferns expressed his horror:

> "Your Grace has, with great concern, observed that our false faithless brother Dunboyne has put the finishing hand to his treachery, by solemnly abjuring the sacred doctrine of that holy church, which had too meekly and patiently suffered the withered rotten limb to adhere to the body for which he was so badly fitted. He now laughs at you all, but his woes and weeping cannot be far off."[23]

---

[21] PTAD, I, No. 18.
[22] A.P.F., S.C., Irlanda, vol. 16, f. 301.
[23] PTAD, I, No. 31, 2.

Dr Dunne had even more sensational news, with the rumour that the apostate was to be made a spiritual peer:

> "The infamous Dunboyne is the hero of every conversation, it is rumoured, that he is to succeed Beresford,[24] who, it is said, is to be translated to Ferns. His Grace of Cashel and Earlsfort have pledged themselves to make him a spiritual peer. He was escorted to his apostasy by all the Tipperarian nobility and gentry. By the bye, they got no great acquisition. His horrors in Cork now begin to transpire. Entre nous the clergy of that city seem to me very reprehensible for winking at his glaring immoralities for their stories are now mustard after meat."[25]

The *Cork Hibernian Chronicle* on 25 August carried this more sober report of the occurrence, with a suggestion that there had been some speculation about his lordship's motives:

> "Lord Dunboyne, the late titular Bishop of Cork, has been the subject of public conversation for some time past, on account of the singularity of his situation. By his marriage he estranged himself from the communion to which he belonged. However, it now appears, he only waited an opportunity to reform, for on Sunday last [19th], in the public church of Clonmel, he went through all the forms prescribed by law and was received into the established Church, in the presence of the Right Hon. Lord Earlsfort and the Prime Sergeant. Lord Dunboyne's fortune has no augmentation by this step, nor did his lordship forfeit an estate, at an early period of life, as was erroneously reported, for his adherence to the Romish church."

The home of the Dunboynes was to be at Dunboyne Castle, in Co. Meath.[26] Not in the old medieval fortress, but in a more recent house close by. This place, recently recovered, had been a seat of the Barons of Dunboyne for over six centuries, a fact of which the bishop would have been most conscious.

Lord Earlsfort, due to his long friendship with Dunboyne, was familiar with the legal endeavours to recover the old Butler property of Kiltinan; further complications were now added to his lordship's affairs when the family of his sister-in-law, Mary, widow of Pierce, commenced litigation against him. Miss McNamara, daughter of George McNamara of Cong, had brought a good dowry with her when she married, but her husband's affairs did not now return even sufficient funds to provide for her income. For some reason, her family blamed the new heir for this discrepancy and started proceedings.

More disturbing for Dunboyne was the conduct of the local parish priest at

---

[24] Hon. William Beresford, Bishop of Ossory, 1782-95.
[25] PTAD, I, No. 32, 2.
[26] Cogan, *Meath*, i, 195.

Dunboyne Castle, Co. Meath. Until recent years it was a convent of the Sisters of the Good Shepherd

Dunboyne. It would seem that Fr. Patrick Smith strongly disapproved of the bishop's resignation from the See of Cork, and when he learnt of his conforming to the Established Church and his marriage, he swore that he would not remain in Dunboyne if Butler came there. When he knew with certainty that Lord and Lady Dunboyne had arrived he deserted his flock, and proclaimed that he would not return to the parish until they had left.

Fr. Smith, after he abandoned the parish, endeavoured to get the appointment of parish priest at Kells when it became vacant. He opposed the cleric nominated by the bishop, and pushed his own claim to such an extent that the Primate suspended him from office. Nonetheless the priest defied his superior, and continued to say mass there. The bishop retaliated by putting the parish under an interdict, and he demanded that the people should recant publicly and barefooted before he would lift the interdict! Dr Troy was asked to request the bishop to abandon these harsh conditions, and after Fr. Smith himself repented publicly on the Ordinary's next parish visitation he was allowed to resume his priestly duties. But he did not get a parish for a year, when he was appointed to Castlepollard.[27]

Despite the publicity given to the marriage and apostasy of the former Bishop of Cork, and the subsequent local disturbance caused by the parish priest of Dunboyne, the effect on the people in general was minimal. Perhaps their isolation from members of the landed class insulated them from judging Bishop Butler by their own standards; the perversion of gentry, for reasons of property, was not uncommon, though it usually reduced their standing in popular estimation. Reporting to Rome, on 20 September 1787, the Archbishop of Cashel claimed that the apostasy "has had little evil effect, and all attribute it not to conviction but to his own evil desires".[28]

Legends about the lord-bishop grew quickly in the fertile minds of the people. He was the subject of many a bawdy joke, or of anecdotes concerning his pride. One such story relates that on an occasion when he was travelling south from Dublin he sent a footman ahead three or four days before to prepare the way. On arrival in a Kildare town, probably Naas, the servant announced to the hotel-keeper that preparation should be made for the arrival of *Mac Feorish Earla Dranaun, Earla Dungbouna of Cushlaun, agus an Baron Mearagh o Kilteynain.* To the surprise of the hotel-keeper only one guest arrived, instead of the expected party of gentry; it would seem that the baron's footman was having a joke by saying in Gaelic "Pierse's son and earl of Drangan, earl Dunboyne of the Castles, and the merry Baron of Kilteynan".[29]

Nor was the apostasy forgotten by the clergy themselves. A year after the event, on 25 June, Fr Bodkin commented on the papal disapproval of the case in a letter to the parish priest of Cashel, while Dr John Lanigan, Cashel-born professor of Scripture, Hebrew and Ecclesiastical History in the Hanoverian College at Pavia, wrote this letter, dated 8 August 1788, to the Archbishop of Cashel:

> 'The unhappy fall of the late Bishop of Cork which has so sensibly afflicted your Grace, is one of those terrible scandals, which cannot be reflected on without horror. It would be difficult to explain the source of so extraordinary an apostasy, were we not instructed by Religion, that mankind has nothing of itself nisi mendacium et peccatum, [except falsehood & sin] and that terrible are the judgements of the Almighty on the sons of men, when abandoning them to the iniquity of their heart, spargit, to speak with St. Austin, Pendes caecitatis super illicitas cupiditates.[30] How afflicting should not this mon-

---

[27] Ibid., 195-6. PTAD, 11, No. 76, No. 116.

[28] *Rep. Novum,* John Kingston, iii, No. 1, 1961-2, 73.

[29] *Cork Hist. Arch. Jn.* xxi, 1915, 101-2. He was Edmond's son; Pierce's nephew. See also *Journal of Kildare Archaeological Society,* Vol. II, 202, for a similar story from Oxford.

[30] Quotation from St. Augustine *The Confessions,* Book 1, ch. XVIII, (ed. Caillau, Tome 25, Paris 1842, P. 26) Eng. Tr. F. Sheed, 1943, p. 22: 'How hidden art Thou, o God the only great, dwelling in silence in the high places, and by thy untiring law sending blindness as the punishment for unlawful lusts.'

The Dunboyne Shield. The Shield is peculiar to the bishop-baron and impales his wife's arms. It is unlikely that he ever used the shield, as it represents him as a bishop with a wife!

strous event be to our poor country, had not the God of mercy given it many Prelates and especially to the Province of Munster, scene of this tragedy, so worthy an Archbishop, who jointly with his confreres, repairs the break made in the walls of Jerusalem, and [upholds] by the arms of virtue and zeal the reputation of the Holy City. May the [Lord] of hearts grant to that miserable object of compassion the spirit of compunction and repentance, whereby acknowledging the enormity of his guilt and imploring the Divine Mercy, he may obtain Pardon from the Almighty and forgiveness from the Church, which he has so grievously offended."[31]

---

[31] CBACE, 168.

In his *Ecclesiastical History of Ireland to 1829* the Rev. M.J. Brenan outlines the career of Dr William Coppinger, who returned to Cork from Paris about 1780 and was appointed curate to the parish of St Finbarr by Bishop John Butler. Soon he was advanced to vicar-general of the diocese, and parish priest of Passage. Commenting on the defection of the bishop, Fr. Brenan wrote: "[it] occasioned, as may be expected, an unusual degree of scandal; in Passage the affliction was severely felt, but the unremitted zeal and charity of its good pastor supplied the people with paramount consolation".

Nevertheless, the extraordinary conduct of the Bishop of Cork is not quite so outrageous when seen in the historical context of 18th century Ireland. While his ecclesiastical and social position made the perversion more sensational than the frequent apostatising of clerics and lay folk, there were many other strange occurrences to divert the public.

A glance through the newspapers for 1788 gives some indication of happenings which involved Catholics, as reported in a mainly Protestant press.

By far the most sensational happening of the period was the trial of Rev. Patrick Fay for "uttering a receipt knowing it to be forged, with an intent of defrauding Patrick Fulham". He was convicted and condemned to be executed, and on the night of 7 November "the ropes were out all night at the New Prison, and all the frightful apparatus displayed for the intended execution. Mr Fay has been attended constantly by Rev. Mr. Gamble, and appears to be very fervent in his devotion".[32] A few days later the *Dublin Evening Post* summarised Fay's history; the son of poor parents from Co. Meath, he had been taught Latin, and went to the continent to study for the priesthood. After ordination Fr. Fay was appointed chaplain to a French man-of-war, and "amassed about one thousand pounds". He returned to Ireland, but in September 1772, at Navan, recanted from Popery, and was awarded £40 a year, the usual allowance for ecclesiastical reformists. For a time he held the appointment of chaplain to the Royal Hospital, Kilmainham, but was expelled for misconduct. He was next active as a "couple-beggar", or clergyman who performed marriages for runaway or hasty couples, and the ex-priest was so described in a newspaper report in October 1786 when he was accused of "assaulting and wantonly abusing Bridget Duffy, a poor woman". He was found guilty, but on paying restitution, his sentence was mitigated.

The Catholic authorities had him excommunicated, but instead of being daunted by this calamity, Fay acquired a wife, a widow with property, and still continued to function as a "couple-beggar". He was also a developer, and when "the old Piazzas" in Essex Street, Dublin, were demolished, he built houses there. Now, however, while he was in New Prison, his tenants availed of his absence, and did not pay their rents, and he was in a miserable condition in-

---

[32] Brady, *18th c. Press,* 262-3, 266, 268.

deed. Then on 13 June 1789, he was carried on the open Kilmainham cart to the brig *Duchess of Leinster,* for transportation to Maryland. Fay now disappeared from the Dublin scene until 1795 when he was apprehended in Dublin, and again lodged in New Prison. Though he appealed for a discharge, he was committed to prison to suffer the sentence passed on him seven years before.[33]

There were worse tragedies than Fay's. In 1788 a priest in Bandon was thrown from "a skittish horse", and killed,[34] while a Drogheda priest was found dead, "sitting in a chair, his head leaning on his hands, and is imagined to have been in that situation two days".[35] Worse was the fate of the parish priest of Knockantowry, near Cashel. While asleep he was murdered by his maid-servant, who absconded.[36] A much more trivial event caused the Rev. Lynch, of Denmark St chapel, to appear in the columns of the *Dublin Evening Post.*[37] While saying mass in the chapel his "umbrella was stolen by some sacrilegious wretch, who made a clear escape with the theft undiscovered".

There was good news too. The Augustinians in Creagh Lane, in Dublin, got a new organ, the first to be introduced to a chapel in the City.[38] At Straffan, in Co. Kildare, a handsome chapel was opened at the expense of the local landlord,[39] and a new licensed school for Catholic children was ready to open in Limerick.[40] In Liffey Street chapel, in Dublin, a Sunday school was being held,[41] and on 26 July the graves in St. James's Churchyard, in Dublin, were decorated with garlands and flowers. This annual custom had, in previous years, been the cause of riots and disturbance, but in 1788 it passed quietly.[42]

The Rev. Fr Arthur O'Leary, the noted Capuchin author, was presented to the king at a levee, and complimented on "his candid and philanthropic writings",[43] and a short time later the *Cork Journal* informed the public that Dr O'Leary's pension had been again granted, as it had been stopped when he had a literary quarrel with the Bishop of Cloyne.[44]

Clergy continued to apostatise themselves. In June, a priest of Strabane parish read his recantation and preached to a large congregation on the text "there is more joy in heaven over one sinner that repenteth, than over ninety

---

[33] Brady, *18th c. Press,* 294, 296.
[34] Ibid., 259.
[35] Ibid., 261.
[36] Ibid., 259.
[37] Ibid., 262.
[38] Ibid., 261.
[39] Ibid., 260.
[40] Ibid., 263.
[41] Ibid., 259.
[42] Ibid., 260.
[43] Ibid., 260.
[44] Brady, *18th c. Press,* 261.

and nine persons who need not repentance".[45] Just before Christmas, in Cloyne Cathedral, the Rev. John M'Mahon was received into the established church.[46]

In Cork, a few days after Christmas, two men were committed to the county gaol for "publishing at the chapel at Currikeepane, at the head of a large congregation, an inflammatory letter from Captain Right the parishioners to pay money which was accordingly levied".[47]

So ended another year, an uneventful one for Lord and Lady Dunboyne, as far as is know. For the next few years Lord and Lady Dunboyne lived the quiet life of gentlefolk in their country home, possibly concentrating on the principal purpose of their union, the production of an heir to the title and estates. Their summers were spent at Gracefield, their six-acre retreat at Balbriggan.

Perhaps his lordship devoted some time to his library. One item from it, the 17th century manuscript of three Irish texts *Forus Feasa ar Eirinn, Tri Bior-Ghaoilne An Bhais* and *Eochair-Sgiath an Aifrinn,* inscribed with the name Lord John Butler, is preserved in the Royal Irish Academy.[48]

Gracefield, Balbriggan, now a Loreto Convent. The bow-fronted section was the Dunboyne's summer residence

---

[45] Ibid., 260.
[46] Ibid., 263.
[47] Ibid., 263.
[48] RIA, MS. 676.

Dunboyne was kind to his tenants, generous to his friends, and charitable to the destitute who were as plentiful as ever. Now that he was legally wed his interest in the established church appears to have declined. He did not attend service in the village, and on a couple of occasions declined invitations to ordinations in Trinity College, Dublin.[49] Nor did he indicate any ambition for a Protestant bishopric. At the time of his apostasy it was rumoured that one of his motives was to gain a rich Anglican See, and his friend Lord Earlsfort, according to a letter in the Dublin Diocesan Archives, promised that he would be considered for such an honour.[50]

One anecdote, of which there are a few versions, about Lord Dunboyne would indicate that the expression "once a priest, a priest for ever" applied to him, even after some years of married life. Dunboyne was travelling through a town one day when a man fell from a roof, and was seriously hurt. His lordship, seeing the grave situation of the injured man, alighted and gave him absolution. While this story is recorded in the *History of the Diocese of Meath*,[51] a later historian added a codicil which claims that the injured man recovered consciousness to see the one-eyed face close to his; he thought his last hour had come, and called out "it is the devil", no doubt to claim a victim! However, appropriate and all as the anecdote is, it may not be factual. A similar story is told about Archbishop Miler Magrath, the 16th century apostate, when the prelate is said to have encountered his victim near Golden, not far from Cashel.

Another version of the Dunboyne story places the accident in the hunting field. A beater, sheltering under a ditch, was jumped on by a horse, and seriously injured. Lord Dunboyne, who was mounted, descended from his horse and prepared to give the man absolution. He was horrified when the injured man cried that he would rather go straight to the other world as he was, than take absolution from the ex-bishop. The rebuff was believed to have indicated to Lord Dunboyne the horror in which he was held by the people, and it started him thinking about his circumstances.[52]

The late Eoin O'Mahony told yet another variation of the story :

> "Butler was driving along a country road when a woman rushed out of a house calling for a priest for a dying man. Butler heard the sick man's confession, but was severely reprimanded by his pious coachman who told him he was nothing but an apostate priest. This plain talk appears to have affected him deeply".[53]

---

[49] England, *Life,* 226.

[50] PTAD, *Minutes,* 20. 12. 1801.

[51] Cogan, *Meath,* i, 197.

[52] Information from Sr. Rita O'Donoghue, Sacred Heart Convent, Mount Anvil, Dublin, 14.5.1975.

[53] *Butler Jn.,* Eoin O'Mahony, ii, 1969, 88-89.

In the Loreto Convent, Balbriggan, which was then the Dunboyne's summer lodge, a similar story is told, but this time the injured man was lying on the beach, and he died comforted by Dunboyne.[54]

---

[54] Information from Sr. M. Benedict, Loreto Convent, Balbriggan, 12.1.1976.

CHAPTER FOUR

Remorse and Repentance

The uneventful life of the Dunboyne's was sometimes enlivened by a visit from a relative or neighbour, and occasionally from a stranger, introduced by a friend. Such a person was Charles Bowden, an Englishman travelling in Ireland to collect material for a book on the island.

When Charles Bowden returned home to England, and wrote down his impression of Ireland, this is what he had to say of the Dunboynes whom he had met at Clonmel, through a Mr Moore:

> "Her ladyship is certainly a most angelic creature, though her fine form at that time, by an advanced state of pregnancy, appeared rather to disadvantage. His lordship is extremely affable and much esteemed by all his acquaintances. It is imagined he will shortly be called to the House of Lords, either as a spiritual or a temporal peer."[1]

While the writer's latter surmisation proved incorrect, his description of Lady Dunboyne is interesting. And he was kind to his lordship, who has been elsewhere described as "a stupid man, blind of an eye, with a sinister countenance".[2] At Wilford there is a tradition that Lady Dunboyne gave birth to a premature infant, which was buried in the Augustinian friary at Fethard.[3]

As the days slipped into weeks and months, Lord Dunboyne fell into a deep depression and he decided to try the diversion of Dublin city. Dunboyne Castle was leased and a townhouse rented from Mr Leeson, in the new street named after the successful brewer himself, Leeson Street.

The apostate bishop's conduct was now something of a *cause célèbre*, though as four years had elapsed since his inheritance the subject was no longer of burning interest, even in Cork. The knighting of Henry Browne Hayes, Sheriff of Cork, in 1790 was of more concern in that city, as he was a colourful character who had married well, built himself an imposing mansion on a hill-top near Douglas, and was now rearing his children without the aid of his wife, who had left him and returned home to her family. Or the latest grave-robbery,

---

[1] Bowden, Charles, *Tour through Ireland*, 1791, 156.
[2] Madden, D.O., *Revelations of Ireland*, 1877, 34.
[3] Information from Barrys of Wilford, 12.12.1975.

18 Leeson Street, Dublin, where Lord Dunboyne died. Until recent years it was a convent of the Sacred Heart Order

in the cause of science, would create a temporary stir, particularly if the robbers were apprehended. However, in the month of June 1790 the affairs of John Butler would again have roused the public imagination when one of his former priests wrote a strongly worded letter to a London paper.

Dr Arthur O'Leary O.F.M. Cap., from near Dunmanway, Co. Cork, was yet another controversial cleric in that age of controversial clerics. He had been educated at St Malo, and after ordination remained there until 1771 as chaplain to the prisons and hospitals, the inmates of which included many Irish soldiers. In that year he returned to Cork and helped in founding a chapel for his order in Blackamore Lane, under the authority of Bishop Butler.[4] Soon his sermons attracted great crowds, and his outspoken pamphlets attacking Whiteboyism created controversy. One of his other publications *The Divinity of Christ,* was in reply to what he considered "a blasphemous work by a Scottish physician in Cork"; he sought the Protestant bishop's permission to issue that pamphlet. In

---

[4] Walsh, *Nagle*, 21.

1789, almost three years after Bishop Butler apostatised, Dr O'Leary left Cork and settled in London. But he had not abandoned the limelight, and when in the following year he was wrongly accused of having himself deserted the Roman Catholic church he sent a spirited letter to a newspaper, of which this is an excerpt:

> "I do not consider Lord Dunboyne as a model after whom I should copy. With his silver locks, and at an age when persons who had devoted themselves to the service of the altar in their early days, should, like the Emperor Charles the V., rather think of their coffins than the nuptial bed, that prelate married a young woman. Whether the glowing love of truth, or Hymen's torch, induced him to change the Roman Pontifical for the book of Common Prayer, and the Psalms he and I often sung together, for a bridal hymn, his own conscience is the best competent to determine. Certain, however, it is, that if the charms of the fair sex can captivate an old bishop to such a degree as to induce him to renounce his breviary; similar motives, and the prospect of aggrandisement, may induce a young ecclesiastic to change his cassock.
>
> Having, from my early days, accustomed myself to get the mastery over ambition and love, the two passions that in every age have enslaved the greatest heroes, your correspondent may rest assured, that I am not one of the trio mentioned in his letter."[5]

Dr O'Leary's rumoured defection was based on his attendance at a Protestant service, with the permission of the parson and gentry, to address a number of discontented Catholics who had gone there with the intention of conforming. *The Dublin Evening Post* of 14 September 1786 considered "this singular anecdote of a Roman Catholic clergyman's going to the church for the preservation of order, and of the Protestant magistrates going to the chapels for the same purpose, to be the death-warrant of bigotry and fanaticism in the kingdom".

Perhaps it was Dr O'Leary's letter which inspired an anonymous poet to pen a new ballad on Lord Dunboyne in the autumn of 1790. Entitled *Lord Dunboyne's Reformation* it vilified both Lord and Lady Dunboyne, suggesting that he was drunken and lustful, while Maria deceived him with other lovers. Even his loss of an eye provided inspiration for the cruel satirist; part of the poem went as follows:[6]

> Hail, Lord Dunboyne, you nobly play'd your part
> You fix'd your fame and gratified your heart.

---

[5] England, *Life*, 222-3.
[6] Copied from a manuscript dated 12.10.1790 in the library of St. Patrick's College Maynooth, by Rev. P. Corkery, PP Rathowen, Co. Westmeath, to whom I am indebted for this copy.

Fear not the prelates h[ate] the Estateman's sneer
The ladies tatler or the layman's geer [sic].
Enough for you while drunk with lust and wine
To flirt and wanton with your concubine.
Think not of scandals, scandals there must be
Or why a Judas, or a sot like thee.
Too long, my Lord, Religious mark you bore
Too long the crosier or the mitre wore.
A Cross to you has been an irksome load
Altho' made holy by a bleeding God.
The wiley [sic] hypocrite you've acted long
'Tis fine to be the theme of ev'ry tongue.
Your proud deeds to future lines should run
And every clime your gallantry must own . . .
Since every age affords not one like you
The Devil grieves no doubt that Bishops fall so few.
But oh! take care, tho' Puss you can beguile
Whilst you please'r her, faith she can beguile.
Instead of one, had you got Argos' eyes
Or had you watch'd'r with a thousand spies
The old and impotent she will deceive
And your new pulpit to other preachers give.
You need not fear an heir to your Estate
Or Heaven averted antlers to your pate.
Set Man and Angels see that you can do
As much to torture Christ as Turk or Jew.
But oh! keep Judas in your mental eye
Lest Judas-like you hang yourself high.

Even Charles Etienne Coquebert de Montbret, the French Consul in Ireland, describing his travels through the country in 1791, remarked of Dunboyne village:

> "the place from which one branch of the Butler family derives its title. The present lord, who had been the Catholic Bishop of Cork, took it into his head to become a Protestant in the hope, it is said, of acquiring children and a Protestant bishopric – with no success in either case".[7]

In the same year Lord Dunboyne must have been disturbed to read a report in the *Dublin Chronicle* of 17 September which reported that just a week before "[e]leven persons, who had gone to [a Protestant] church to see a neighbour's child married, and partook of the bridal feast, were obliged to perform public penance in the North Chapel, standing in white sheets, as a warning to others

---

[7] *Journal Kildare Archaeological Society*, Síle ní Chinnéide, XV, 1974-5, 383.

how they should dare to profane themselves, by going within the walls of a church, or partake of heretical food." What, he might ask, would be his own penance if he repented?

During the last decade of the 18th century many historic events happened in Ireland. The United Irishmen were formed in 1791, and in April of the same year the first convict ship sailed from Cork for Australia. Wolfe Tone made his appearance on the political stage; Lord Edward FitzGerald discovered a different kind of patriotism to that of his family, which occupied a position in Kildare comparable to that of the Butlers in Kilkenny. Lord Dunboyne did not take part in any of the political happenings, and we do not know his views on them. He would have been conscious of the importance of the establishment of a college to educate men for the priesthood at Carlow in 1793, and he may have followed with interest the planning, and eventual opening of Maynooth College two years later.

Pilgrimages, held secretly during the Penal times, were again observed publicly, and in the year that Maynooth opened there was a major boating accident on Lough Derg. A ferry-boat *en route* to the holy island foundered in ten feet of water and ninety pilgrims were lost. Though the accident happened not far offshore the onlookers were so horrified they failed to take out the available rescue boats. However, one of the priests on the island "ran to the shore and gave conditional absolution to those drowning". It was rumoured that, even at the early hour on a Sunday morning when the tragedy occurred, the principal boatman was under the influence of drink.[8]

One morning, in the month of May 1794, Lord Dunboyne took a stroll from Leeson Street, through St Stephen's Green to the Clarendon market. There, to his surprise, he met an old acquaintance, Edward Sheehy, from Charleville, accompanied by a fourteen-year-old youth.[9] Dunboyne was pleased to encounter an old friend who did not appear to hold any resentment against him, though he was taken aback when Sheehy mentioned that he had heard the rumour that his lordship had been offered a seat in the House of Lords. Sheehy introduced the youth to Dunboyne as James Butler, his sister Bridget's son, and a grand-nephew of Archbishop James Butler of Cashel, and a Butler of the Dunboyne line. Lord Dunboyne invited Sheehy to bring the boy to breakfast in Leeson Street the following morning, but there is no further evidence of any further meetings between the parties.

It would seem that Lord Dunboyne's efforts to provide an heir were to be futile; he was described as "a slave to family importance; and he grieved to find himself the last barren link of a long and distinguished race".[10] In 1795 the Dunboyne's suffered a double family bereavement when Maria's father and her

---

[8] O'Connor, D., *St. Patrick's Purgatory*, 1931, 180-2.
[9] *Rep. Novum,* Sir Henry Blackhall, iii, No. 2, 1963-4, 372-3.
[10] England, *Life,* 225.

older sister, Mrs William Butler of Park, died on the same day in the month of March. They were buried in the family vault at Drom, near Templemore.

Back in Cork, life went on as usual. But sometimes there was the unusual, in 1797 Sir Henry Browne Hayes, having been made a widower some years before, decided to find himself another rich wife. Undeterred by the execution of the Kilkenny abductors Strange and Byrne some years before,[11] Browne Hayes abducted his chosen bride, a Quaker heiress named Pike, and a "couple-beggar" priest was procured to perform the marriage ceremony. But the bride was retrieved, and Browne Hayes went on the run. Eventually he was apprehended and transported to Australia.[12]

1798 brought greater political unrest, culminating in the Rebellion. Bishop Moylan of Cork issued pastoral instructions "to his beloved flock, and in particular to the lower order of the Roman Catholic inhabitants of the diocese", in April. He exhorted them "to endure whatever portion of evil the general distribution of Providence may fall to their share. Certain privileges excepted, you possess the advantages of the constitution. The Penal Laws, under which our fathers groaned have been almost all done away with. I know that efforts have been made by evil minded men to weaken your allegiance to the best of Kings, but, in the name of God, why should you be the dupes and tools of those wicked incendaries?"[13]

Nevertheless, in June "one Neal, a man of £400 a year, was hanged at Cork, for being concerned with 36 others in the murder of a poor soldier". According to the *Freeman's Journal* Neal was brother to the priest of Ballamacoda, who had also been punished for treasonable practices.[14]

As the Dunboynes were still resident in Dublin in 1798 the rebellion did not greatly affect them. But the lord's old friend, Dr William Gahan OSA, of John's Lane, Dublin, was seriously injured by the military during their search in that area for Lord Edward FitzGerald.[15] Dunboyne village was burnt down by the troops, and the little chapel destroyed. When Butler learned of this he offered the parish priest, Fr James Connell, a site for a new chapel. The men were already on amicable terms, but Dunboyne died before his offer could be formalised. However, according to Rev A.Cogan's *History of Meath,* the Butler family did provide the site for the new chapel when it was built.[16]

Another story told about the former bishop further indicates that he did not hold any animosity towards the church. During a visit to Tipperary the priest of Killusty, near Fethard, interceded with Lord Dunboyne for assistance.

[11] Weiner, Margery, *Matters of Felony,* 1967.

[12] *Trial of Sir Henry Browne Hayes, bart.* Cork, 1801. Australian Encyclopaedia.

[13] Moylan, Bishop, *Pastoral Instructions,* Cork, 1798.

[14] Brady, *18th c. Press,* 304.

[15] *Rep. Novum.* John Kingston, iii, No. 1, 1961-2, 75.

[16] Cogan, *Meath.* i, 197.

Bishop Butler's chalice, dated 1621, which he presented to the parish priest of Killusty.
It is still in the parish church of Fethard and Killusty

Some time later, when the priest thought that his request had been ignored, his lordship arrived at his door and handed him a cloth-wrapped gift. It was a chalice dated 1621. "Here is a chalice for you with which I often celebrated mass in happier days, take it from my polluted hands", cried the unhappy old man.[17] The vessel is still preserved at Fethard.

Lord Dunboyne's conscience would seem to have been troubling him. His apostasy had been in vain, his marriage barren, and now, in his sixty-ninth year, his health was failing. More and more he longed for reconciliation with Rome,

[17] *Rep. Novum*, John Kingston, iii, No. 1, 1961-2, 74.

and eventually he decided to write to the Holy Father. In April 1800 he was ill, but when he recovered somewhat he wrote two letters which he asked his physician, Dr Purcell, to be delivered to Archbishop Troy of Dublin.[18] One of the letters was intended for the Pope, and the other, for the archbishop, told of Dunboyne's illness and desire for reconciliation. The letter to Rome, dated 2 May, read as follows, in translation from the original Latin:

> 'Here, prostrate at the feet of Your Holiness, is that most unhappy Jn Br formerly bishop of Cork in Ireland, who, having left his episcopal See, without permission, joined in an impious marriage with a heretical woman. Fearing lest he be heaped with ecclesiastical censures and penalties, he took himself – in a worse crime – to the side of the heretics. Now, tho' belated, led by, as I hope, true repentance, I most humbly beseech your Holiness that once again I be allowed into the fold of the True Church and absolved from all reserved sins.
>
> I shall put forward no excuse nor, I confess, could I, for such great crimes, but because of human weakness, I may be allowed to recount the following ones. I am the last in the direct line, from an illustrious family which never forsook the true religion and furthermore despoiled of almost all its inheritance and about to be despoiled of the remainder if I were to die without an heir, while I was contesting, at enormous expense, an unjust judgment.
>
> All these years I was trying to put an end to this litigation but in vain even to the very end, as they say, in which I accepted the final sentence. And if I hadn't accepted I would have been unable either to give a decent endowment to the woman joined to me, or to reserve anything for my own modest sustenance. And on account of the vain hope of an heir I was prolonging from year to year the time of my return to the Catholic Church. Excepting the first day when I was received into the assembly of the heretics I have entered no temple to assist or administer the Sacred Rites excepting an Oratory once to assist. I received no Sacrament or Catholic rite.
>
> With my spouse I have had no cohabitation, except at table, for more than five years; nor can I assert absolutely that she is other than a virgin, altho' we have always up to this lived in mutual benevolence and love. Nevertheless I am ready to fulfil manfully whatever Your Holiness decides about me. Meanwhile I earnestly pray the great and good God to long keep your Holiness safe and well. Your most Obedient and most humble servant".
>
> Dublin this second day
> of the month of May, 1800.
> John Butler, Baron Dunboyne,
> formerly Bishop of Cork.[19]

---

[18] Gahan, *Testimony*, 5.
[19] A.P.F., S.C., Irlanda, 17, f. 668-9.

On the day before he wrote to the Pope the dying nobleman had made his
Will, an action which was to lead to much recrimination when the contents of
the document became known.

Archbishop Troy arranged for the transmission of the baron's supplicatory
letter to Rome, but he prudently decided to take immediate action himself
also. Knowing of the friendship between Dunboyne, when he was Ordinary of
Cork, and the devotional writer Dr William Gahan OSA, he asked the friar to
call on the penitent.[20] Dr Gahan, a former provincial of the Irish Augustinians,
was at this time one of the best-known religious writers of the English-speaking
world, having published books on Catholic devotions, the history of the church,
an exposition of the catechism "for the Use of Grown-up Children and other
illiterate Persons" and, a couple of years before, "Youth Instructed in the Grounds
of the Christian Religion, with remarks on the writings of Voltaire, Rousseau,
T. Paine etc." He had established a school in John's Lane, Dublin in 1777, not
far from Old Broad St, where he had been born in 1732.[21] Dr Gahan knew his
lordship of old, having visited him in Cork in 1783. They had remained on
cordial terms and corresponded. When Dr Gahan, as provincial of his Order,
planned to attend a Chapter in Rome in 1786, he consulted with the Bishop of
Cork.[22] That was also the year in which Butler inherited his title, and from then
until now there had been no contact between them.

When the friar presented himself at the Dunboyne residence in Leeson St,
as directed, he was amused to find that the man-servant mistook him for a
medical man when he gave his name as Dr Gahan.[23] In fact, it was later rumoured that Lady Dunboyne had instructed that no Catholic priest was to be
admitted, and that Dr Gahan, with the aid of a servant, was disguised as a
physician come to visit.[24] Tradition further embellished this audience with a
miracle! Fr Gahan, it seems, was reluctant to absolve the penitent too easily,
and said that he could not impart forgiveness until such time as rivers ran uphill.
Dunboyne wept so much at this stricture his tears ran up over his forehead, and
back on to, his pillow. This extraordinary display of grief satisfied the friar, and
he confessed the old man.[25] Another version of that tale was set at Wilford, but
there it was perspiration which channelled his forehead – like the river before
the old house.[26] *Walker's Hibernian Magazine*, dated May 1800 carried in its
death notices the short news "died at his residence in Leeson Street, the Rt.
Hon. Lord Dunboyne". Behind this information was hidden the drama of the

---

[20] Gahan, *Testimony*, 6.

[21] Martin, F.X. OSA, *Dictionnaire de Spiritualité*, vi, 1965, 69-70.

[22] Fenning, *Undoing*, 330.

[23] Gahan, *Testimony*, 9.

[24] *Bell, The*, XXV, 1951-2, 37.

[25] Tradition from the late Mons. Maurice Browne, PP Ballymore Eustace, 29.9.1975.

[26] Tradition from Barry's of Wilford, 12.12.1975.

former Bishop of Cork's last days, and his death on 7 May. But the shroud of silence was not long to lie over the circumstances of the passing of this extraordinary gentleman. Within a year his final wishes would be subjected to the scrutiny of the Court of Chancery, and before another year was out his private deathbed conversations and intentions would provide material for common gossip.

Naturally, the hierarchy was interested in the death also, as is evidenced in a letter, dated 24 May, from the Archbishop of Cashel to the Bishop of Cork, in which the writer mentions that he had "written to-day to Dr. Troy to favour me with the particulars of Lord Dunboyne's death and last Will".[27]

Though the national newspapers recorded the death of Lord Dunboyne, they gave no further information on the funeral arrangements and burial. It might have been expected that he would be laid to rest at Dunboyne, but this was not so. However, in the records of the ancient Augustinian friary at Fethard, Co. Tipperary is the following entry: "the late Catholic Bishop of Cork [Butler], who became a pervert to enjoy the title of his family, Lord Dunboyne, is herein interred".[28] But this record only dates from the 1830's, when a visiting Provincial of the Order had been to the friary. It was, however, a traditional burial place for the family, and a Dunboyne monument, dated 1619, is still to be seen there, but there is now no indication of the bishop's burial place.[29]

Oral tradition of the almost secret interment was collected by a priest when writing a history of Fethard friary. It told that on one very snowy day Mrs Mary Kickham, with others, saw coming down the Killenaule road a solitary hearse, with the driver and a woman, wrapped in one of the old fashioned Irish cloaks, seated up beside him in front. They were informed it was the funeral of Bishop Butler (Lord Dunboyne), whose remains were being brought from Shangarry, near Mullinahone, to be buried in the Augustinian Abbey, Fethard. This account raises a number of questions: Snow in May? No mourners? Why should the funeral be from Shangarry? As the *Annals of Fethard* gave no further details, the historian, Fr Kingston, surmised that Dunboyne had been buried near his wife's home at Wilford. Later his faithful sister, Catherine O'Brien Butler, whose sons had inherited much of his property, decided that he should lie in the ancestral vault at Fethard. This accounted for the snow storm, which would have been out of season in May, though not unheard of. The same writer believed that the woman in the Irish cloak was the widow, Mrs O'Brien Butler. [30]

---

[27] *Coll. Hib.*, Evelyn Bolster RSM, No. 14, 1971, 82.

[28] Butler, T.C., OSA, *The Friars of Fethard*, 1976, 32.

[29] Knowles, J.A. OSA, *Annals of Fethard*, 1903, 136.

[30] *Rep. Novum*, John Kingston, iii, No. 1, 1961-2, 77. Tradition from Fr. J. Butler, OSA, Grantstown, 19.12.1975.

*The Sanctuary of the Augustinian Church, Fethard, beneath which Lord Dunboyne
was interred*

Another complication to the story was added by an Augustinian writing
some seventy years ago. He noted that "Fr. Gahan attended the funeral obse-
quies of the repentant bishop in the abbey of Fethard",[31] and it has even been
suggested elsewhere that the friar was disguised in the Irish cloak![32]

In 1800 the friary ruins were owned by the Lowe family, though some
friars lived close-by in a thatched cottage. The ruins were recovered by the
Augustinians in 1820, and partly restored. When Fr James Anderson was there
later in the century the Dunboyne memorials were moved. Even by then confusion had arisen about the Butlers, and Fr Anderson wrote "Bishop Butler, the
last Lord Dunboyne *and author of the catechism* was a descendant of . . .".[33]

Definite proof of the burial was found in 1935 when a new sanctuary was
being laid down. Beneath the little chapel known as "the Dunboyne" a vault
was found containing lead coffins, two of which were identified as belonging to

[31] Knowles, J.A. OSA, *Annals of Fethard*, 1903, 139.
[32] Tradition from Fr. T.C. Butler, OSA, Grantstown, 19.12.1975.
[33] *Seanchas Ardmacha*, Catherine M. Dwyer, vii, No.2, 1974,248.

the Dunboyne family. One of them was that of the bishop-baron, and the other that "of his only child, a daughter", who had been buried beside him.

Significantly, the remains of Lord Dunboyne had been placed feet towards the altar, while the child's head was in that direction. The traditional practice of burying priests with their heads towards the East, to signify that they were the heralds of the Gospel, was extended to baptised infants who would be seen in the same light. But whoever was responsible for the burial of the bishop-baron did not consider him worthy of the normal honour, and this would seem to indicate that a priest officiated at the entombment.

An old man who was present at the opening of the vault over forty years ago recalled a tradition that after the bishop had been entombed in 1800 "his followers armed with swords and pistols guarded the vault to prevent the coffin being removed by the people of Fethard, who strongly voiced their indignation at its being buried in the sanctuary".[34]

But what about the daughter? After a visit to Rome in 1964 the late Eoin O'Mahony sent the following note to Lord Dunboyne:

> "I always thought that Bishop Lord Dunboyne of Cork had no children but for some reason or other they are taking great interest in him in Rome at the present time, and I learned that the bishop's tomb in Co. Tipperary was recently opened and that a tiny coffin was found there. It is believed that this is the coffin of a baby born to the bishop. As you know he spent ten years waiting for a dispensation to become a priest. This was necessary because he had only one eye. The latest in Rome is that it was knocked out in a riot in a tavern."[35]

Whether Eoin O'Mahony's surmise and the Wilford tradition about John Butler's posterity is correct or not may never be proven, as the inscriptions on the coffins were not recorded. They lie in peace beneath "the Dunboyne", though the chapel has since been dedicated to Our Lady of Good Counsel.[36]

---

[34] Butler, T.C., OSA, *The Friars of Fethard*, 1976, 26,32,34.
[35] Note from Eoin O'Mahony to Lord Dunboyne, 5.4.1964.
[36] Butler, T.C., OSA, *The Friars of Fethard*, 1976,22.

CHAPTER FIVE

The Trial at Trim

While Maria Butler, Lady Dunboyne, may have been disappointed in her fourteen years of marriage, and her failure either to produce an heir, or secure the title for her brother, she may have had some solace from the conditions of her husband's Will[1] which she and another executor proved. "To my dearly beloved wife" he left all his furniture and effects in their Leeson Street home; financially she was to be provided for life from the rents of certain lands in Tipperary, while the O'Brien Butlers, his heirs-at-law, inherited after his death. To the Royal College of Maynooth, then just five years old, Lord Dunboyne bequeathed Dunboyne Castle and village, after the death of his sister Catherine. This was the bequest concerning which the Archbishop of Dublin had asked Dr Gahan to consult Dunboyne, and now, it seemed, that Dr Troy's worst fears were to be realised.

The fact that Baron Dunboyne had left his castle to the Catholic college does not seem to have prejudiced the O'Brien Butlers unduly. Two of the men, Pierce and Edmund, lived in Bansha and, in the usual fashion of that period, their upbringing was in the Protestant church, the religion of their father. Nevertheless, they were active in encouraging the building of a chapel in Bansha, and not only did they donate a site, but they also helped with subscriptions.[2] Their mother, however, who was a Catholic, and the only surviving member of the late Lord Dunboyne's family, was not pleased that Maynooth should gain from the Will. She was convinced that the Will was unjust to her as heir-at-law and that she herself was deprived of income by the settlement. She put her case before the Lord Chancellor, Lord Redesdale, on 31 October 1800, claiming that the Archbishop of Dublin had forced her brother to make the Maynooth bequest, as a penance for his apostasy.[3] Her principal legal argument, in an effort to prove that the Will was illegal, she based on the conditions of the 1793 Relief Act. This Act, she insisted, benefited Catholics, but did not concern Protestants. They were still subject to the old Penal Law, Mrs O'Brien Butler held, which forbade them to will property if they had become Catholics. The fact that her brother had embraced Protestantism was well known, and as

---

[1] *Index to the Prerogative Mills of Ireland 1536-1810*. Ed. Sir Arthur Vicars, 1897, 148.

[2] *Rep. Novum,* John Kingston, iii, No. 1, 1961-2, 78.

[3] Gahan, *Testimony*, 3.

he had again become a Catholic on his death-bed it meant that his Will was void. Even in death John Butler was to continue to cause gossip and scandal.

Lord Clare took a keen interest in the proceedings, and had dealings with the archbishop. Clare was of the opinion that the Relief Act had been intended to remove all disabilities of the Penal Laws, including the clause affecting converts from Protestantism. The case was brought before the Chancery Court in 1801, when Dr Gahan made no less than six separate appearances before the court. His evidence was vital to the case, as only he was in a position to say whether, in fact, Lord Dunboyne had died a Catholic or a Protestant. As the friar considered himself bound by the seal of the confessional he refused to divulge his conversations with the penitent. The Master of the Rolls decided to transfer the case to the Meath County Assizes, scheduled to be held in Trim, in the month of August 1802.

Lord Kilwarden, the Lord Chief Justice, was on the bench when the case, *Catherine O'Brien Butler, Plaintiff, versus the Rev. A. Dunn, Secretary to Maynooth College*,[4] opened at Trim Assizes on 24 August. Arthur Wolfe, 1st Viscount Kilwarden, was at this time one of the most distinguished members of the judiciary; a man of humanity and dignity, he maintained his reputation for integrity even during the 1798 period. He was eloquent in the defence of his namesake and family associate Theobald Wolfe Tone, a cause which prevented him from being appointed Lord Chancellor in 1802. At the time of the Trim trial he was one of the official visitors to Maynooth College.

The College was represented at the trial by George Ponsonby and John Philpot Curran, the latter one of the most famous Irish barristers of all time, and then a household name as a result of his defence of Fr Neale and of the Sheares brothers. Kilwarden, who had a passion for punning, sometimes referred to Curran as "Gooseberry". Sergeant Moore and Standish O'Grady were counsel for Mrs O'Brien Butler; both were most able men, and O'Grady was later appointed attorney general and a judge. It was indeed a star-studded court, and the issue to be decided was one in which there was considerable public interest. Consequently, as would be expected, the court was packed when the trial commenced. Sergeant Moore summarised the circumstances of the case as follows:

> 'Lord Dunboyne had been born and educated a Catholic, and had attained the rank of a Roman Catholic bishop. Afterwards he had duly conformed to the Protestant religion, and shortly, before his death had relapsed to Popery, and, when weak in his understanding, and under the influence of Catholic Priests, by whom he was constantly visited, had made the Will in question, by which he disinherited his sister, who was his heir-at-law, and her children, and left his estate in the County Meath to the Roman Catholic College of

---

4 Gahan, *Testimony*, 3. PTAD, Green file, I, No. 39.

Maynooth, having been induced to consider such devise as a meritorious act, and the price of his reconciliation, with an offended God. By the laws now in force, a person relapsing to Popery from the Protestant religion, was deprived of the benefit of the laws made in favour of Roman Catholics, and was, of course, as under the old Popery laws, incapable of making a Will of landed property."[5]

While the defence admitted that the late Lord Dunboyne was absolute owner of the land, and that Mrs O'Brien Butler was his heir-at-law, it was denied that he had been under any influence whatsoever when making his Will, at which time his understanding was perfect. Mr Ponsonby, who was making this plea, observed that whenever a public body benefited from a bequest the question of hardship to the heirs was always raised: "if such an outcry was attended to, neither here nor in England should we have to boast of those numerous charitable and public institutions, which formed the pride of each country. Why should a bequest to Maynooth not be as good and valid as one to the Lying-in Hospital, Simpson's Hospital, Steven's Hospital and such?". Next the Will of Lord Dunboyne was proved, by one of those who had witnessed it, and it was further proved by the same person that the testator was of sound mind at the time.

The Archbishop of Dublin, Most Rev. Dr Troy, travelled to Trim to testify that he had received two letters from Dunboyne, asking to be received back into communion with the Church of Rome. One of the letters was to be sent to the Pope, and in it Lord Dunboyne expressed sorrow for having abandoned the faith and broken his vows as a bishop. Dr Troy emphasised that he had twice written to the testator advising that his property should be left to his family, and not to Maynooth. If it was his intention to leave something, as a mark of his sincerity in returning to the church, the archbishop had advised, it would be as well done by a small legacy as by giving away part of his inheritance.[6]

To quote Fr Kingston, historian of the Dunboyne inheritance, "the O'Brien Butlers now produced an extraordinary witness, a maid in the house at Leeson Street, who professed to be a Catholic". This servant maid, as she is termed in the published account of the case, swore that Fr Gahan had frequently visited the deceased in his last illness. "On one visit", she said, "when the priest left the room at about midday, there was a candle lighted on the table, and a small round silver box". Lord Dunboyne, from his bed, requested the maid to bring him the box, which he put under his pillow. When asked if she were a Catholic, the woman said yes, and she also admitted that it was usual to have candles lighting when the sacrament was administered.[7]

---

5 Gahan, *Testimony*, 3, 4.
6 Gahan, *Testimony*, 5, 6.
7 Gahan, *Testimony*, 6.

The next, and principal, witness Dr William Gahan, was already a popular figure, due to his spiritual writings and pulpit eloquence. By this time the friar was feeling tired of the whole Dunboyne business, and pleaded that "since last December I have punctually and obediently attended six painful examinations concerning the cause still pending, and with no small inconvenience I have undertaken a journey to this remote town,[8] and present myself here this day to testify my obedience and respect for this honourable court". Then he satisfied himself that the oath which he was to take ("The evidence you will give …") would leave him free, as a priest, to demur, as it did lawyers and attorneys not to feel bound to disclose the secrets of their clients. The doctor also informed. the court that his title, though an empty one and not carrying any temporal

THE

INTREPID

AND TRULY

Orthodox Testimony

GIVEN BY THE

Rev. WILLIAM GAHAN,

At the Trim Assizes, Aug. 24th, 1802,

Wherein the Lease of CATHERINE O'BRIEN BUTLER,
was Plaintiff, and the Rev. A. Dunne, Sec.
to the Roman Catholic College of
Maynooth, Defendant.

DUBLIN:

Printed by T. & M. Haydock, 17, L. Ormond Quay,

Oct. 18th. 1823.

Price, plain 6d.—with Portrait 10d.

The title pages of the pamphlet The Intrepid and Truly Orthodox Testimony of Rev. William Gahan given at the Trim Assizes in August 1802. *Printed in Dublin in 1823*

---

[8] Tradition from the Liberties, in Dublin, claimed that he travelled to Trim by donkey; from the late Miss Maura Tallon, 19.12.1974.

emolument, he thought proper to mention "in order to suppress the appellation Father Gahan, which a female witness had introduced earlier". He did not wish to hear the term taken up from her, and frequently repeated in a public court.

Mr O'Grady, counsel for the plaintiff, examined Dr Gahan,[9] and having established that the priest had visited and conversed privately and confidentially with Baron Dunboyne, asked the witness if he had had any conversation with his lordship, on spiritual matters.

"I did Sir, it's usual when priests are in company together to speak of spiritual affairs", replied the Augustinian.

"You acknowledge then, that Lord Dunboyne was a priest at that time?"

"Yes, for once a priest, forever a priest, the character of the Christian priesthood being indelible".

Now the counsel endeavoured to clarify the evidence of the maid servant, and having established the secrecy of the bedchamber, the question of the lighted candle was explored.

"Could Lord Dunboyne see without the light of a candle?" was the first question, to which Dr Gahan answered "he was blind of one eye, and whether he could see well with the other eye or not, I could not decide, even though I had been introduced into Lord Dunboyne's house in the quality of a physician I do not presume to be an oculist".

While this reply amused the crowd, it did not satisfy Counsellor O'Grady.

"Can you yourself see without the light of a candle?"

"I never visited Lord Dunboyne at night, being no great admirer of works of darkness. Had I visited him at night, I might have stood in the need of the light of a candle, and of spectacles also. However, in the open day-light I can see tolerably well without the light of a candle, though one would be apt to think that the brilliance of Mr O'Grady's eminent talents and the splendour of his eloquence might be sufficient to dazzle the tender eyes of a man upwards of seventy years old".

"Do you say that upon your oath", quipped the counsellor.

"No sir, it was a thought that just occurred to me, and I threw it out by way of a parenthesis".

"Now Dr Gahan, could you please tell the court if at any time during the last illness of Lord Dunboyne you saw a candle lighting in his bed-chamber?"

"I have never seen any candle whatsoever lighting in Lord Dunboyne's bed-chamber when I was there".

"Could you tell the court, Dr Gahan, if it is usual to have a candle lighting when the Sacrament of the Eucharist is administered according to the rites of the Roman Catholic Church?"

"Sir, it is usual to have candles lighted during the administration of the sacrament, as emblems of the light of the gospel. But it is not essential, and may

---

9 Gahan, *Testimony*, 6.

be dispensed with for proper reasons. It is now, in my opinion, high time to put out the candle."

"While I appreciate your opinion, Dr Gahan, it is my duty to the plaintiff to prove my case, and I must persist in questioning you on this matter. Would you be kind enough to say if you have administered the Sacrament to many sick or dying persons, and if ever you have done so without the light of a candle?"

"I have given the Sacrament to a great number of sick and dying persons when I was a curate at St. Paul's, Arran Quay, in Dublin, some forty years ago. I cannot remember if I administered it to any of them without a lighted candle, when one could be easily procured".

"Do you remember whether you did or did not administer the Sacrament to any person without the light of a candle in the year 1800, at or about the time that Lord Dunboyne was in his last illness?"

"Sir, whether I do or do not recollect such a thing, and whether in my capacity as a priest I do or do not know anything about the matter, I believe I am not at liberty to tell. However, I may say that I never saw, touched or made any use of the communion-box which the female witness has claimed that she found on the table and handed to Lord Dunboyne".

"Dr Gahan, you are my witness, but you seem to give evidence on the other side".

"My evidence is the real truth, and I solemnly declare that I am not interested in the present cause, nor unduly influenced by any of the contending parties; nor would I willingly tell a simple lie on this occasion in order to put the Roman Catholic college of Maynooth in full possession of the two estates of the late Lord Dunboyne".[10]

Mr O'Grady now asked if any masses had been offered for the soul of Lord Dunboyne, and Dr Gahan said he did not know of any, though he himself had offered private prayers for the spiritual comfort and happy death of his lordship.

Then the vital question came: Did the priest know if Dunboyne had died in communion with the Catholic Church?

"As a priest", replied the friar, "I know nothing of the matter; if, indeed, in my capacity as a Roman Catholic clergyman I did know anything of the matter I feel that I am neither bound nor at liberty to disclose it. As I do not wish the court to consider that I am just being unco-operative, may I beg leave to explain my words, lest they be misunderstood?"

"Certainly do, Dr Gahan", said Lord Kilwarden.

"My Lord, gentlemen; when priests of the Roman Catholic Church are juridically examined in circumstances such as this, a rule is laid down for them. It is, to give always uniformly the same answer, in order to prevent the unfavourable conjectures that might be drawn from their silence. Theologians have prescribed that the answer which a priest should give is 'that he knows nothing

---

[10] Gahan, *Testimony*, 13.

of the matter', and this way of answering is accepted in Catholic countries, as priests are supposed to have no human knowledge of the matter concerned, but only the knowledge which they have as ministers of Christ. In the courts of this country, without an explanation such as this, my answer might be looked upon as perjury".

The eloquent address evoked a murmur of approval from the body of the court, causing the judge to call for order before Mr O'Grady could continue with his questioning.

"While you have expressed your situation, as you see it, most ably Dr Gahan, there are a few other points I would like to clear. During the illness of the late Lord Dunboyne did you ever see any other priest or minister with him?".

"Never".

"Sir, this court desires to know did Lord Dunboyne die as a Protestant or a Roman Catholic. As you were on the most intimate terms with him before his death, I now ask you, did his lordship belong to the Reformed Church or the Church of Rome when he died?"

It was obvious to the onlookers that the friar was visibly upset by this direct questioning, which indicated that his earlier plea was being ignored. Now he spoke with passion, and obvious sincerity.

"If I say that Lord Dunboyne died as a Protestant I do not think that I will be believed, rather I will be thought a perjurer. I fear that the world, which is always too quick to judge rashly, may say that the lord died neither one thing nor the other, that he finished his career in impenitence. Consequently I wish to remain silent. I cannot answer that question, but I do not wish my silence to be taken as consent that he received the Sacrament of the Roman Catholic Church. I act only from principle and from motives of conscience".[11]

"Dr Gahan, you place yourself in a dangerous legal position if you persist in demurring".

"I have no wish to be difficult. As a priest I have no option but to be silent".

"Do you wish to take advice from your solicitor?"

"I have no legal representative".

"Your refusal to give information to the court constitutes contempt for this assembly".

"God forbid that I should show contempt for this court! Since last December I have punctually and obediently attended six painful examinations concerning this cause. . . ."

"I appreciate your loyal expressions, but I would now like you to answer plainly, did Lord Dunboyne tell you at any time during his last illness what religious persuasion he was of, whether a Protestant or a Roman Catholic?"

---

[11] Gahan, *Testimony*, 15.

"That question I cannot answer".

Mr O'Grady saw that further questioning of the priest was hopeless. He turned to the judge: "My Lord, you have heard the eloquence of this conscientious doctor. I myself am doubtful as to the validity of Dr Gahan's position, but I request that the court be asked to express an opinion on the matter".

Lord Kilwarden tried to extract an answer from the friar, to no avail: "My Lord, I am grievously upset; I have no wish to show you, or this court, any disrespect. I cannot answer this question further than I have already done".

"Dr Gahan, in refusing to answer you are, in my opinion, guilty of a contempt of court. However, I open the question to the learned men here present on both sides of the court, or indeed to anyone in the courtroom, who would like to stand up and prove to me that I am wrong in saying that the Reverend William Gahan is guilty of contempt of court".[12]

Mr Ponsonby took up the judge's challenge, and rose to speak: "My Lord Justice, I submit that if the reverend gentleman answered the question put to him he might incriminate himself. By the existing laws any person assisting another to pervert from the Protestant to the Roman Catholic Church is subject to severe penalties. He is not bound to place himself in that position by further answering the question".[13]

Philpot Curran, Ponsortby's partner in the counsel for the Secretary to Maynooth College, supported this line of argument with an elegant speech: "I agree with Mr. Ponsonby, and it's my opinion that the witness is not bound in law to disclose anything told to him in confidence as a Roman Catholic clergyman. Our laws protect an attorney or counsel in a case from being obliged to give evidence on matters communicated to them in the cause of their clients. It's my understanding that the religion of this country is part of its law, and that the Roman Catholic religion, as to the practice of it, is as much under the protection of the law as is the Protestant religion. I do not believe that either a Protestant or a Catholic clergyman may be obliged to give evidence of such matters, and I am doubtful indeed that Dr Gahan is bound by law to answer. It is apparent that this reverend gentleman's conduct has been as a result of this principle, and not as a disrespect to this Court. His conduct, I submit, is more worthy of applause and respect than to be rewarded by punishment".

This address greatly pleased the public, but Lord Kilwarden remained unimpressed.

"Despite the clarity of your eloquence, Mr Curran, I remain unconverted in my opinion that Mr Gahan is bound by law to answer the question of the court. In refusing this answer I hold that he is guilty of contempt, and for this refusal I have no option but to sentence him. I now sentence you, Dr Gahan, to one week's confinement in the gaol of this town".

---

[12] Gahan, *Testimony*, 16.
[13] Gahan, *Testimony*, 17.

"My lord, I am grievously upset by not being able to satisfy the court, but I wish to state that I have no interest in the event of the cause, I act only on principle. If, instead of a week's imprisonment, I was to forfeit my life at this moment, I would, without hesitation, be unable to give any answer other than that which I have given".

Again the court showed its approval of the friar's sentiments, but the judge hurriedly ordered the sheriff to escort Gahan to the gaol. As he left the courthouse there were boos and shouts, both inside and outside the building. Lord Kilwarden called for silence, and asked that the next witness for the plaintiff be called.

The document containing Baron Dunboyne's name as one of those who took the Oath of Allegiance as a Catholic at the assizes of Clonmel in 1778 was produced by a clerk from the Roll's Office; he also exhibited an attested copy of the Minister's certificate of Lord Dunboyne's conformity to the Protestant religion. (In the Calendar of Convert Rolls, preserved in the Dublin Public Records Office it is recorded that he signed the certificate on 19 August, and enrolment was made on 9 November.)

Philpot Curran now raised an interesting problem, on behalf of the defendant. He held that Lord Dunboyne had never legally become a Protestant, and consequently never relapsed into the Catholic Religion. His argument was that the certificate signed by Dunboyne in St. Mary's, Clonmel, was invalid as it was improperly worded, and not sealed by the minister, as the law required. His late lordship, Curran contended, having taken the Oath of Allegiance as a Catholic, had every right to make the Will in question.[14]

It was now necessary for counsel for the plaintiff to refute this opinion, and O'Grady hastened to do so.

"My lord, while I agree with my learned friend that there are some small discrepancies in the certificate of Lord Dunboyne's conformity to the Protestant religion, I submit that they are only minor. It is clear that the intention of the lord was to conform, and the witnessing minister certified the proceedings, as he believed to be, accurately. I do not believe that the certificate was essentially bad".

The complexities of the case now caused Lord Kilwarden to direct that "all the facts should be found in the shape of a special verdict, and that a case should be presented at the next term of the Court of King's Bench".

In the meantime, on the evidence heard it was decided that Lord Dunboyne had died a Catholic. With this issue resolved, Lord Kilwarden observed that "as the plaintiff has not suffered by Mr Gahan's refusal to answer the particular question put to him, and as it was very clear that he acted only from principle and not from disrespect to the Court, I do not consider him an object for punishment, and as the dignity of the law has been sufficiently vindicated by his

---

[14] Gahan, *Testimony*, 21.

committal, I now order that he be released from gaol". Dr Gahan had spent one week in confinement.[15] A full account of the trial appeared in the *Freeman's Journal* on 4 September 1802, and a few years later it was reprinted as a pamphlet in London.[16]

The good friar was immediately set free, and returned to his friary in Dublin.[17] There he continued his preaching and writing, and published in the following year "A Short and Easy Method to Discern the True Religion from all Sects". For a second period he served as prior of the Dublin community, until his death, at the age of 72, just before Christmas 1804. He was buried in the Protestant St James's cemetery. But his memory lived on, not only in the stories which were told about his priestly courage at Trim, but also in his many writings which were regularly reprinted for over a hundred years. The Fenian leader, John Devoy, recorded that, as a youth, he sought spiritual solace from *Gahan's Sermons and Moral Discourses*. A living memorial to the Augustinian is the school in John's Lane, Dublin, which still thrives two-hundred years after he established it, now catering for mildly-handicapped children.

Within a year of the trial Lord Kilwarden was dead. On the night of 23 July 1803, during the rising organised by Robert Emmet, Kilwarden and his great-nephew, Rev Richard Straubenzie Wolfe, were being driven through Thomas Street in Dublin when their coach was halted, and the two gentlemen assassinated. The murder, it was believed, was a mistake. It was Judge Carleton (who had condemned the Brothers Sheares in 1798) that the rebels intended to kill.[18]

---

[15] *Notes and Queries*, 5th series, XI, 25 January 1879, 70.

[16] Gahan, *Testimony*.

[17] In Dublin's Liberties tradition claimed that on his return to the city his prior, a Corkman, reprimanded him in connection with the court case. Insulted, Dr. Gahan walked out, assumed lay garb and went into lodgings in Brick street. From Miss Maura Tallon, 19.12.1974.

[18] *Journal Co. Kildare Archaeological Society*. 1899-1902. III. 365.

CHAPTER SIX

The Settlement

Misinformation about Dunboyne's bequest to Maynooth persisted into the late nineteenth century. W. Maziere Brady in his *Episcopal Succession in England, Scotland and Ireland 1400-1875*, wrote that "Lord Dunboyne left most of his property to Maynooth College, where he founded bourses, which still bear his name", while Augustus Jesop, DD, in *Notes and Queries* (5th Series, 1879) said that Dunboyne "left a large sum to Maynooth College, where his name quâ peer, is revered, quâ Protestant pervert, is abhorred."

The terms of Lord Dunboyne's Will which caused his sister to bring the case to court were those which bequeathed his property in Meath (worth £1,000 a year) to the Trustees of Maynooth College, to be applied, after his sister's death, as they should think fit for the benefit of the college. The bequest was subject to an annuity of £200 a year to Lady Dunboyne. At the end of the Trim trial Lord Kilwarden had recommended the case to the next term for the Court of Queen's Bench. But he further advised that, as an alternative, the parties should endeavour to reach an amicable settlement. This advice was accepted, and there was no further litigation. Before the Dunboyne heirs and Maynooth College were able to reach a settlement it was necessary for a special Act of Parliament to be passed in 1808. The Act, (48 George III, c. 145) enabled the Trustees of Maynooth to compromise the suit. With Bishop Sughrue of Kerry, in a letter dated 6 December 1805, to Bishop Moylan of Cork, one might now ask the question: "I understand the trustees of Maynooth have come to a compromise with the heirs of Dunboyne. How much does the College get, and how is it to be disposed of?"[1]

The result of this law was that the income from part of the Dunboyne estate, amounting to a sum of £500 per annum, would come to the College, to be applied exclusively to the Dunboyne Establishment. The Government agreed to give £700 a year towards the Establishment, which additional sum enabled twenty students to be admitted. The purpose of the Establishment was "to maintain and endow selected scholars for additional studies", each of whom was to get £30 a year, and to be provided with fire and candles.[2] In 1813 a special

---

[1] *Coll. Hib.*, Evelyn Bolster RSM, No. 15, 1972, 72. PRO, MS 875.
[2] Healy, *Maynooth*, 300-309. 8 and 9 Victoria, 30.6.1845.

Dunboyne House, St. Patrick's College, Maynooth, completed in 1815

residence, known as Dunboyne House, was built, and in 1820 a Constitution was drawn up for the regulation of the Establishment. "The twenty selected students ought to excel the other students not only in knowledge and intellectual endowments, but likewise in the purity of their life and morals.[3] They would remain in Dunboyne House for three years, during which time they could be required to fill the places of absent professors with the other students. They had a separate table for themselves in the dining hall, and a distinguishing dress. This was described as "a cloak, or toga, somewhat similar to that worn by the professors and superiors".

They could have tea for breakfast, at their own expense, and they could walk in the country in a body twice a week; a prefect or monitor was answerable for their conduct whilst abroad. Their syllabus of studies included the defence, in the presence of the trustees and the entire community, of a thesis in Latin, and the preaching of a sermon before the college on a feast day. Dunboyne students were held in the highest esteem, and their successful completion of the course was regarded as equivalent to taking a degree in other countries. On graduation the students were generally regarded as Doctors of Divinity, and usually addressed as such.[4] Though now changed in character, the Dunboyne Establishment is still part of the University at Maynooth, and as such it keeps

---

[3] Healy, *Maynooth,* 306.
[4] Ibid., 308.

alive the name of its founder in a way which would surely have been agreeable to him.

Nor did the title of Lord Dunboyne become extinct with the death of the repentant bishop of Cork. When his sister, Mrs O'Brien Butler, died in 1804, her son had the ownership of Dunboyne Castle, and it remained in that family's possession until 1859. But they did not have the title, and when one of them endeavoured to claim the lordship in 1823 he was not successful.[5]

James Butler,[6] the youth whom Mr Sheehy had introduced to the 22nd Baron in 1794, petitioned the Lord Lieutenant claiming to be Lord Baron of Dunboyne.[7] In 1827 he legally acquired the titles, and the present Lord Dunboyne is of that line; it was to that branch of the family that archbishop James Butler I, who had consecrated John Butler as Bishop of Cork, also belonged. In fact, if Archbishop James had outlived Bishop John he would have succeeded to the family title, but he had died, aged 83, in 1774.

Maria, the widow of the former bishop, survived him by sixty years. In the September of the year following Dunboyne's death she married again, at the age of thirty-six.[8] Her husband was 35 year-old John Hubert Moore, who had an estate of over a hundred acres at Shannon Grove in Co. Galway.[9] Having served four years as an army officer, Moore had entered the Middle Temple in London in 1787. He studied at the King's Inns prior to being called to the Bar in 1792.[10] His rooms were at Cuffe St and later at St Stephen's Green in Dublin.[11] In this marriage she was more fortunate, and gave birth to a son in 1805; he was christened Hubert Butler Moore.[12] Again, tradition has further dramatised Maria's story: it was said that one day, while pregnant, she drove a tinker-woman, who was also pregnant, from Shannon Grove. The tinker cursed her, and when Lady Dunboyne's baby was born it had neither legs nor arms. Nevertheless, the infant was believed to have prospered, and as an adult entered Parliament.[13] However, this is in the realm of folklore, and is but one of many such tales.[14]

Lady Dunboyne was again widowed in 1822 when John Hubert, who was

---

[5] *Com. Peerage*, iv, 1916, 519.
[6] James Butler of Cragnagowra, Co. Clare had married in 1779, Bridget daughter of Bartholomew Sheehy of Drumcullholer, Co. Limerick, and it was their son, James, who succeeded as heir-male of Bishop John.
[7] National Library, MS 496.
[8] *Annual Register, etc.*, 1801, 52.
[9] Burke's Peerage, 1849, 336. Walford, E., *County Families of the United Kingdom, 1864*, 708.
[10] *Memorials*, King's Inns Library, Dublin.
[11] *The Treble Almanack*, Dublin 1801, 118.
[12] Walford's *County Families of the United Kingdom, 1864*, 708, errs in claiming that Hubert Butler Moore was the 'second but eldest surviving son' of the marriage.
[13] Tradition from Fr. J. Curtis, OSA, Fethard, 12.12.1975.
[14] *ARV, Journal of Scandinavian Folklore*, XXIX-XXX, 1973-4. Sean Ó Súilleabháin, 36-49.

Shannon Grove, near Banagher, where Lady Dunboyne lived out her life

a year younger than herself, died. [15] Their son Hubert attended Trinity College to study law, and he married Mary Blake from Co. Galway in 1824,[16] and soon Lady Dunboyne was a grandmother. But she had her share of sorrows, burying her daughter-in-law at the age of 32, and two infant grandaughters; her only grandson, Capt. Butler Dunboyne of the 89th Regiment, pre-deceased her by five months in 1860, when he was aged but 38.[17]

The Moore's home was a pleasant two-storied house with big windows and a porch with a charming fanlight. Great yews sheltered the house, which looked across flat parkland to the Shannon. Two large reception rooms flanked the hall, and the circular staircase at the back of the house had a decorated ceiling, alcoves and coloured glass in the windows.

Though the Moores have long left Shannon Grove, Lady Dunboyne is still remembered there. The present owner recalls old tales which tell of the hearing of the swish of the skirts of a ghostly Maria climbing the stairs, and the place where her ladyship sat, beneath an elm near the orchard, is still pointed out.[18] While Lady Dunboyne's summer-house has disappeared from the neglected garden, her old seat is preserved. The long avenue to Shannon Grove seems to have changed little since her time, and in years gone by it was believed that the

---

[15] *The Treble Almanack,* Dublin 1822, 148.
[16] Walford, E. *County Families of the United Kingdom, 1864,* 708.
[17] Moore family tomb inscriptions, Clonfert; *Burke's Landed Gentry of Ireland. 1912.*
[18] Tradition from Mrs. K. Finney, Shannon Grove, 8.12.1976.

avenue was haunted.

When Lady Dunboyne died in 1860 she was buried in the cemetery at nearby Clonfert Cathedral in a tomb surmounted with an elaborate sarcophagus decorated with the family Arms, and surrounded with ornamental railings. The inscription reads:

> 'To the memory of MARIA Dowager LADY DUNBOYNE who died 6 August 1860. Aged 95 years. This monument is inscribed with Reverent Affection by her only Son HUBERT BUTLER MOORE of Shannon Grove in this Parish.'

The inclusion of Butler in her son's names indicates that she felt proud of her former name. He was a magistrate for his county in 1852. One of his four children and only son was named Butler Dunboyne Moore, which proves that the family did not hold any ill-will against the barren bishop. The descendants of Butler Dunboyne Moore's daughters still flourish.

Did John Butler, Lord Dunboyne and Bishop of Cork win the final battle?. At first, it would seem, he did not. The sad admission in the final paragraph of his last letter to the Pope indicates the futility of his marriage.

This strange personality was not subdued by death, and a century later his spirit was still wandering around 18 Lower Leeson St, then a convent of the Sacred Heart Order. [19] The sisters had purchased the house, which was slow to sell, as it had a reputation of being haunted. The nuns did not fear the next world, and occupied. the house happily until their Provincial came on a visit from England. Mother Digby, who died in England in 1911, had been converted to the Roman Catholic Church due to "an experience" which has not been divulged. It was believed that, before conversion, she was a bigoted Protestant. During her visitation to Leeson St, her health was poor, and she was raised by lift to the first floor of the convent, to a room close to the chapel. This room was traditionally considered to have been the late Lady Dunboyne's boudoir, and it was while sleeping there that the long dead former bishop appeared to the nun. He was dressed in riding kit, an unlikely garb for a restless spirit seeking consolation. He asked that masses and prayers should be offered for him, and the Sacred Heart Provincial saw that these intercessions were made. After a while the ghost appeared again to Mother Digby to inform her that now his soul was at peace, and to thank her for her interest in his predicament. Mother Digby, according to the records and traditions of her Order, was a lady of common sense, and not given to romantic fancy.[20] Nor has Maynooth College forgotten its benefactor; as late as 1974 it acquired, at auction in Clonmel,

---

[19] Previous owners included Chief Justice T.L Lefroy, who passed sentence on John Mitchell in 1848, and Lord Ardilaun, who was living there in 1883.

[20] Tradition, from Sr. M. Henry, Sacred Heart Convent, Monkstown, 14.5.1975.

a sideboard which was once the property of the errant bishop;[21] and it also received the prayer book, "said to have been used by the baron during his weird apostasy", the words of the present Lord Dunboyne, who gave the memento to the college. He himself treasures "the wedding ring which caused all the trouble".[22] The bishop-baron's gold pectoral cross, of the reliquary type, and decorated with the emblems of the Passion, used to be displayed in the college museum.[23] Unfortunately, it was among the items not recovered after a robbery there some years ago. This loss has been somewhat compensated for by the acquisition of the inscribed brass candelabrum, from the South Chapel, Cork.

No portrait of Dunboyne now hangs in the college, and the story that the students mutilated his image in disgust is an unlikely one. In 1786 when he perverted, the college was not yet founded, and in 1800, on his death, though the institution was not anxious to benefit from his endowment, it is doubtful the students would have behaved with such vehemence, even if St Patrick's College had displayed a portrait of a prelate who had resigned almost ten years before it was established.

---

[21] Rev. Tomás Ó Fiach, President, St. Patrick's College, Maynooth, in a letter to writer, 30.6.1975.

[22] Dunboyne, Lord, *Butler Family History*, 1966, 21.

[23] *Third An Tostal Catalogue to the Museum of St. Patrick's College, Maynooth*, 1955. Item 523.

CHAPTER SEVEN

Postscript

Today John Butler's name is scarcely remembered in the places where he lived. Grange, near Fethard, where he was born is marked by a low ruined house, with the remains of an older church nearby. Kiltinan castle, which his family and himself sought to recover, still stands dramatically above the Clashawley river at the end of a fine oak avenue. But the Cookes are no longer the inhabitants, having followed the local Butlers into oblivion.

While Fr Butler was parish priest of Ardmayle he lodged with the Strangs of Colleagh in their fine three-storied and thatched farmhouse, attached to an old castle.[1] Now long reduced to two stories, and slated, the house nestles amongst great trees, and the story of the bishop is but vaguely remembered by the Ryans, who own Colleagh.

In Cork city there is no record of the house at Monkstown in which Dr. Butler lived. At Pope's Quay the house which was formerly No. 50, and now named St. Mary's, still retains its 18th century appearance, and the hall and stairs have panelling of the period; it may have been Bishop Butler's residence. One place in the city which he certainly knew is the South Chapel in Dunbar Street. Now much restored, it was built in 1766, during Butler's episcopacy, and he probably blessed it.

St. Mary's Church, Clonmel, the scene of the Bishop of Cork's apostasy and, most likely, of his marriage, has been restored in the last century. Of the extraordinary events of 1787 there is now no record in the church registers, nor any knowledge amongst the parish dignitaries.

Wilford, the house where Lady Dunboyne was born, is full of charm, though a ruin. Situated on a tree-dotted slope above the King's River, the mansion was a shallow rectangle, with octagonal towers at each end. Before the fires in those cosy tower-rooms Maria Butler spent her girlhood, and possibly learnt of her forthcoming marriage to his lordship. Locally Wilford is known as "the bishop's house", and Maria has been reduced to the status of maidservant![2] All three houses in Leinster in which Lord and Lady Dunboyne lived became convents. Dunboyne Castle, an attractive 18th century mansion, became a hostel under

---

[1] *Rep. Novum* John Kingston, iii, No. 1, 1961-2, 66.
[2] Tradition, from Barry's of Wilford, 12.12.1975.

the care of the Sisters of the Good Shepherd, but it is now again in private ownership. The compact shooting-lodge at Balbriggan, where the Dunboynes spent part of the summer months, now enjoys its sea view across the railway line, and forms the nucleus of the Loreto convent. The house in Leeson Street (now No. 18), Dublin, where Lord Dunboyne died, where his ghost was said to have been seen by a nun, was a convent of the Sacred Heart Order, but it is now transformed into offices. In each of the three religious orders once associated with the Dunboyne houses there is some memory of his strange, sad story, and it was an old nun who was long familiar with the rooms in which the Dunboynes lived out their lives, and who had a keen interest in their story, that sealed this tale for me: "Dunboyne may not have had an heir, but the unhappiness of his final years was sufficient punishment for his pride. The Establishment in Maynooth continues his name, and through it he has done immense good for many boys, and for the Church. God must be pleased with him, and has forgiven him, and so should we."

Lord Dunboyne's Will

In the name of God. Amen, I John Butler, Lord Dunboyne, being sound in mind and body do make my last will and testament hoping in the mercy of Almighty God to obtain pardon thro the passion of our Redeemer Jesus Christ of my sins, and when it pleaseth Almighty God to call me out of this world my will is that my remains be interred without any show or pomp in a private manner, and not until visible signs marks of my dissolution appear. I leave and bequeath all my estates and lands of and in the Co. of Tipperary, viz. Grangebeg, Killavalla, woods of Killavalla and commons thereunto annexed Bolea Turin and Castletown by the various names by which they have heretofore been known with all other my estate and lands in the county Meath viz. Dunboyne castle and demesne, the castle farm, the grange and all and every of the denominations of ground thereunto adjoining divers houses and messuages in the town of Dunboyne and neighbourhood of Priestown, Riestown and the sub-denominations, the codeens and all other denominations of grounds now in my possession or that shall be in my possession at the time of my death, in either of the said counties or in any other city or county or town in Ireland with all my rights, titles or interest, As or in any other property I may acquire or have a just claim or title or in or to every building thereon unto Edward Lee of the city of Dublin Esq. Counsellor at law, the Rev. Usher Lee of the city of Waterford clerke and unto the survivor of them and the heirs or assigns of such survivor for ever upon trust to and for the uses intents and purposes following that is to say that they the said Trustees Edwd. Lee and Usher Lee clerke or the survivor of them and the heirs or assigns of such survivor do and shall from time to time and after my decease recover sue for or receive all rents issues and profits of said several lands and premises and thereout pay to my dearly beloved wife Maria Butler otherwise Lady Dunboyne for and during her natural life one annuity or yearly rent charge of £600 sterling in case I shall have no issue by her that shall attain the age of 21 years and in bar of all dower or thirds of my real or personal property saving what I shall hereafter express payable by two half yearly payments on the 25th day of March and 29th day of September in each year the first payment thereof to be made on the 25th day of March or 29th day of Sept. next after my decease in case I shall have no issue by her who may attain the age of 21 years the sum of £400 sterling payable after the same manner either of which annuity or rent charges respectively by me bequeathed to her is to be for her own sole and separate use and benefit and I order and direct that no part thereof shall be paid to no other person but to my said wife and upon her own receipt and none other my intention being that no other receipt shall be sufficient at any time, any person for the same and that such annuity and rent charges or any part thereof shall by no means be in any manner under the disposal, controul, or subject to the intermeddling of any persons she shall hereafter marry after my decease her coverture notwithstanding and I order and direct that my said wife shall not mortgage or sell such annuity or rent charge or any part thereof and that if she be prevailed on to do so such sale or mortgage shall be void, and that such annuity or rent charge shall be paid and laid out and expended for her own sole and separate use and none other as if such sale or mortgage had not been made and in case such annuity or rent charge or any part thereof shall be in arrear or unpaid to my said wife or any of the times of payment aforesaid I do hereby authorize and empower her and her attorney lawfully authorized to enter upon any aforesaid lands and premises and to destrain for the same and to dispose of such distresses according to law until fully paid and satisfied such annuity or rent charge and all arrears and costs that shall attend such proceeding as in such cases is usual, I term subject to such annuity to my beloved wife as aforesaid I desire my said Trustees to convey assign and make over all my said estates real freehold and personal and all my lands and premises as aforesaid and all my rights titles and interests therein to such issue as I shall have by my said wife in manner following that is to say if my said issue shall be a son, then and in such case to and for the use of such son his heirs and assigns for ever upon his attaining the age of 21 years and not before. And if I should have more sons than one to the eldest of such sons his heirs and assigns for ever who is always to take in preference to the younger sons according to seniority of age and priority of birth. And if I should leave a son who should die under the age of 21 years leaving issue male, then I leave and bequeath my estates of what nature or kind soever the said issue male upon his attaining the age of 21 years as aforesaid and his heirs and assigns for ever. But in case I should leave a son who should die under the age of 21 years leaving issue female then and in such case I leave and bequeath all my estates of what nature or kind soever in the county of Tipperary or elsewhere (except my estate in the county of Meath) to said issue female her heirs and assigns for ever, if but one on her attaining the age of 21 years, and if more than one, then and in such case to and among them all share and share alike, their heirs and assigns for ever, to take as tenants in common and not as joint tenants on their respectively attaining the age of 21 years and not before. But if I shall not have a son by my said wife, and shall have a daughter or daughters by her then and in such case I leave and bequeath all my estates real or personal of what nature or kind soever (except my estates in the county of Meath aforesaid) to such daughter, her heirs or assigns for ever. If but one on her attaining the age of 21 years aforesaid, and if more than one, to and among all such daughters, their heirs and assigns for ever on their respectively attaining the age of 21 years as aforesaid to take as tenants in common and not as joint tenants. And I order and direct that my said issue shall not be entitled thereto until he she or they respectively attain the age of 21 years and the rents and profits which shall during that time become due out of my said estates after paying such annuity to Lady Dunboyne as aforesaid are to be applied by my said Trustees or the survivor of them or their heirs or assigns of such survivors in discharging my debts and supporting such issue. And I do hereby appoint my said wife guardian of the persons and fortune of each of such issue but in case I shall not have issue who shall live to attain the age of 21 years then and in such case I leave and bequeath all my several estates lands and premises and my rights titles and interest therein subject to such annuity to Lady Dunboyne as aforesaid unto the following persons viz. my estates and lands in the county of Tipperary that is to say Grangebeg, Killavalla, woods of Killavalla and commons thereunto belonging, Bolea Turin and Castletown by the various names they have heretofore been known (which estate and lands I appoint and direct shall principally and in the first place be restored to and subject to Lady Dunboyne's annuity or rent charge payable thereout of the same will be sufficient) to my said Wife Lady Dunboyne during her natural life, but after her decease and my decease, then I desire that my said Trustees shall out of the issues and profits of my county Tipperary Estates or by sale or mortgage thereof raise a sum of £1000 sterl. to be disposed of in the following manner, that is to say, I leave and bequeath £500 sterling of it to my nephew Pierce O'Brien Butler, his executors, administrators and assigns, and the remaining £500 sterling.I leave and bequeath to my nephew Edmond O'Brien Butler, his executors, administrators and assigns, and from and after the death of Lady Dunboyne and after the said sum of £1000 sterling is so raised by my said Trustees as aforesaid, I then leave and bequeath all my estates in the Co. Tipperary aforesaid to my nephew Morgan or Murragh O'Brien Butler of Bansagh in the county of Tipperary for and during the term of his natural life without impeachment of waste and from and after the determination of that estate then to the use of the Rt. Hon. Hugh Lord Baron Massey and Charles Hamilton of the city of Dublin Esq. and the survivor of them, their heirs and survivors of such assigns during the life of said Murragh or Morgan O'Brien Butler upon trust to support and preserve the contingent uses and estates hereinafter limited from being defeated and destroyed and for this purpose to make entries and bring actions as the case shall require but nevertheless to permit and suffer the said Morgan O'Brien Butler and his assigns during his life to receive and take the rents issues and profits thereof and every part thereof to and for his and their use and benefit and from and after the decease of said Morgan or Murrough O'Brien Butler to the use and behoof of the first son of the said Morgan or Murrough O'Brien Butler and the heirs male of the body of such first son lawfully issuing and in default of such issue then to the use and behoof of the 2nd 3rd 4th 5th and 6th and all and every of the son and sons of the said Morgan or Murrough O'Brien Butler and the heir of the body of such son lawfully issuing severally successively and in remainder one after another as they and every one of them shall lie in seniority of age and priority of birth the elder of such sons and the heir of their bodies. And in case my said nephew Morgan O'Brien Butler should die without issue male then and in such case I leave and bequeath all my estates in the Co. of Tipperary aforesaid unto Pierce O'Brien Butler said Morgan's next brother and his issue male and then in failure of issue male according to the limitations specified with regard to the said Morgan and his issue. And in failure of such issue to my right heirs for ever and in case I should die without issue male, then and in such case I leave and bequeath all my estates in the Co. of Meath, the Castle of Dunboyne and demesne, the castle of Trim and Grange, all my houses and messuages in the town of Dunboyne and neighbourhood, Priestown and with their subdenominations and all other denominations of ground now in my possession in the county of Meath after the death of my sister Catherine O'Brien Butler unto the Trustees appointed by Act of Parliament to the College of St. Patrick Maynooth. But all which estates in the Co. of Meath I hereby charge in the first instance with an additional annuity of jointure of £200 to my wife Lady Dunboyne during her natural life to be paid to herself alone and under the clauses mentioned with regard to the Co. of Tipperary estates which several estates in the counties of Tipperary and Meath are to be subject and liable to all charges and incumbrances affecting the same either by this my last will and testament or in any other manner and to all my debts and legacies provided, I shall not appoint any other fund for the payment of the same and also subject to make good any deficiency that may be requested in order to make up the annuity payable to Lady Dunboyne after she has resorted in the first instance to the estate in the county of Tipperary. Item I leave and bequeath unto Lady Dunboyne all my plate, furniture, horses and carriages that are in my house in Leeson St. Dublin together with said house and all my right title and interest therein provided I shall not have issue of my own to inherit the same to her and her heirs for ever, and in case I shall have issue of my own by my said wife Lady Dunboyne then and in that case I only leave her the use for her natural life of said house in Leeson St. Dublin with remainder to my said issue. And whereas I am entitled to a large property due to me on the estate of Stephen Creagh Butler late of the city of Dublin in case the same be not recovered in my life time, I do order and direct that the executors hereby appointed to this my last will and Testament do carry on the suit now pending and on the recovery of the same and payment and receipt thereof do dispose of the same in the following manner, in the first place I desire that thereout all my bonds notes and all just debts I owe at the time of my death may be discharged. And as a fund will be requesite to carry on the said suit for the recovery of the said money due on the estate of the said Stephen Creagh Butler, I do desire order and appoint that the issues and profits of my estates in the county of Meath, be resorted in the first place and before any other claim any other person may have either by this my last will and Testament, or in any other manner for the supporting and defraying all just and lawful costs shall attend the recovery of the same. Item I leave and bequeath out of the same fund due on the same St. Creagh Butler's property as aforesaid the sum of £500 to Lady Dunboyne. But in case I should die without issue male by my said wife Lady Dunboyne, then and in that case I leave and bequeath the following sums viz. the sum of £3000 to my nephew Morgan or Murrough O'Brien Butler, £100 to the north infirmary of the city of Cork and £50 to the south infirmary of Cork, and £50 to the charitable society for the relief of insolvent debtors in the said city of Cork and £50 to the poor housekeepers in the parish of St. Mary Shandon Cork. I likewise leave to the poor housekeepers of the parish of Fethard in the county of Tipperary £25 and an equal sum to the poor house-keepers of the parish of Kilimane in the same county. Item I do hereby direct and appoint that the aforesaid Trustees Edward Lee and the Rev. Usher Lee and the survivor of them or the heirs or assigns of such survivor after they have in the first instance every year during the life of Lady Dunboyne paid her the additional annuity of £200 a year which I leave by this my will charged to her out of the Meath estate aforesaid, and after they shall have paid all my debts, incumbrances and legacies and fulfilled the other trusts reposed in them do receive and pay my sister Catherine O'Brien Butler during her natural life, should she survive me, all issues and profits of my estate in the county of Meath subject however to all clauses heretofore mentioned, and likewise to any resi-due that may remain after paying all my debts legacies and incumbrances out of the money due by Stephen Creagh Butler and all other personal property I may have or be entitled to at my death, but the above issues and profits of my county Meath estate as well as the above residue of my personal property she is only to receive and be paid on condition that she for herself her heirs executors and administrators and assigns do renounce quit claims to all and every manner of right she may have or imagine she has to any share or part of the money due by Stephen Creagh Butler as being part of the assets of my late brother Pierse Lord Baron Dunboyne or his son my nephew Pierse Edmund Creagh Butler or any other assets belonging to either, as likewise to any legacy or assets belong-ing to my brother Edmund Butler deceased or money were not sufficient to pay the debts and incumbrances they owed and which I have since their deaths paid besides the costs of a very tedious and expensive suit at law for the recov-ery of the assets that did belong to them or and in case she the said Catherine O'Brien Butler shall refuse to renounce as aforesaid every such claim and right she may have or imagine she may have to such assets or legacies and then and in that case I do require and direct my aforesaid Trustees Edward Lee and Usher Lee clerke or the survivor of them or the heirs and assigns of such survivor to pay the issues and profits of my aforesaid estates in the county of Meath subject to all expences my said Trustees may be at, as heretofore mentioned to the Trustees of the Royal College of St. Patrick for the benefit and use of the said college to whom I have before by this last will devised my said estate in the county of Meath after the death of my said sister Catherine O'Brien Butler as aforesaid, and if any residue should remain out of my personal property after paying all my just legacies and incumbrances the same shall remain in the hands of my said Trustees until after their expenses are satisfied, then to be paid to my wife Lady Dunboyne her heirs or assigns, whom I do appoint as my residuary legatee in case my said sister Catherine O'Brien Butler should refuse the same under the above mentioned conditions. item I leave and bequeath £100 to the same Edward Lee one of the above mentioned Trustees with my diamond ring. And I do appoint the said Edward Lee and my said wife Lady Dunboyne executors to this my last will and Testament. In witness whereof I the said John Lord Dunboyne have to this my last will and Testament and to a duplicate thereof of the same date and tenor put my hand and seal this 1st day of May in the year of our Lord 1800.

Dunboyne's seal

Signed sealed published and declared by the testator John.

Lord Dunboyne as and for his last will and Testament in the presence of us who in his presence at his request and in the presence of each other have hereunto subscribed our names as witnesses of the following blanks being first filled up in his own handwriting as he acknowledged only his desire - the blank 19th line first the testator desired to be filled up and the next two lines and half were filled by the testator himself on the third page after the word (unto) as well in the three subsequent three whole lines after the word (Meath) and the two last lines of the same page after the word (they) and the two lines at the 22nd line of the fourth page after the word (mentioned) were all inserted and wrote down by himself.

Thomas Spinner, Thos. Lysaght junior, Edward Edwards

1st May 1800

Copy – Lord Dunboyne's will and signed at the foot Crawford and Grace.

Index